Praise for *The Wise Leader*

Few ideas have more historical connection with leadership than wisdom, and few ideas have lost more currency. In the so-called "knowledge era," wisdom seems to have come out a distant second to technical skills and navigating organizational politics. While important, these cannot possibly substitute for working relentlessly to develop our ability to be aware, to listen from others' points of view, and to discern the short- from long-term consequences of alternative actions. Paul Houston and Stephen Sokolow have had long careers in educational leadership, learning what these capabilities mean in the cauldron of complex issues and embedded conflicts, and we are fortunate that they can now help others find their way onto an authentic path to become a wiser leader.

—Peter Senge, founding chair, Society for
Organizational Learning, and senior lecturer, MIT

"You are looking for knowledge," said the Wizard. "True knowledge (wisdom) comes from experience, and experience you have in plenty." Those paraphrased pearls come from L. Frank Baum's The Wizard of Oz *and are the cornerstone of* The Wise Leader. *Houston and Sokolow unlock the treasure trove of authentic leadership: soul, heart, courage, and grit—all the real spiritual stuff others fail to get. Read, enjoy the inner journey, and experience the rapture of discovering an accumulated personal storehouse of wisdom.*

—Terrence E. Deal, author of *Leading with Soul*
and *Reframing the Path to School Leadership*

I've spent much of my adult life promoting the idea that it's critical for all who lead to "rejoin soul and role," for our own sake and the sake of those we serve. The courage to act wisely and well comes from a set of core values that encourages us to do what is right even when it's easier to do what is expedient. That's why I think The Wise Leader *is an important book. It offers a deep understanding of what these core values are and how they can be accessed in a leader's daily work.*

mer, author of *Healing the Heart of Democracy,*
Let Your Life Speak, and *The Courage to Teach*

T0367462

The need for leaders who are enlightened, principled, and spiritually grounded is greater now more than ever. This powerful book is essential for anyone in any position of responsibility—it not only underscores why doing the right thing is important, but it also provides thoughtful and inspired guidance on how to be a wise, exemplary, and transformational leader.

—Bill Milliken, founder, Communities In Schools, and author of *From the Rearview Mirror* and *The Last Dropout*

Never will you find such a constellation of distilled wisdom on leadership for all circumstances as can be found in Houston and Sokolow's The Wise Leader. *Each of the eighteen core values is distilled into six to twelve elements. My suggestion is that you take one principle a day and dwell on its specific features. In less than three weeks you will know a great deal about effective leadership.*

—Michael Fullan, professor emeritus, OISE/ University of Toronto

The Wise Leader *is brilliant! The authors have created an easily accessible, practical, timely, and timeless approach for navigating the many challenges all leaders face. The key ingredient for this leadership success is rarely identified and perhaps never before put into such a clear, concise, and well-organized framework. In this book the reader will learn how to strengthen the spiritual muscles needed to lift—and even enjoy—the increasingly heavy load placed in front of today's leader.*

—Alan Blankstein, president, HOPE Foundation

The Wise Leader

Doing the Right Things for the Right Reasons

PAUL D. HOUSTON
AND
STEPHEN L. SOKOLOW

edited by Robert W. Cole

iUniverse LLC
Bloomington

THE WISE LEADER
DOING THE RIGHT THINGS FOR THE RIGHT REASONS

iUniverse books may be ordered through booksellers or by contacting:

iUniverse
1663 Liberty Drive
Bloomington, IN 47403
www.iuniverse.com
1-800-Authors (1-800-288-4677)

ISBN: 978-1-4917-1028-9 (sc)
ISBN: 978-1-4917-1030-2 (hc)
ISBN: 978-1-4917-1029-6 (e)

Library of Congress Control Number: 2013917751

Printed in the United States of America.

iUniverse rev. date: 11/4/2013

Table of Contents

This book is dedicated to

Steve's grandchildren,
Gabrielle, Sebastien, and Lyla

and

Paul's grandchildren,
Will, Lucy, and Jade,

who represent our
best and brightest future.

Foreword

From the time I started working on a ship at the age of fourteen I have understood the value of hard work. But my thirty-plus years of working as a leader and helping leaders improve their effectiveness all over the world have helped me understand that working hard is not enough. It's also necessary to work *smart*. And working smart requires internalizing the importance of valuing and empowering others.

Much of my work has been involved with helping others navigate the storms and waves of change that are sweeping across the world. Yet in this environment leaders need to make sure that their organizations are highly productive and proficient. Research has shown that only about one in four employees operates at peak performance. How can leaders improve these dismal statistics? By building a positive organizational climate, a climate in which people *want* to come to work—and that can happen only when leaders value their team members and implement strategies that empower them.

I have written several books on leadership and management, consulted with and coached hundreds of executives, and delivered more than a thousand keynote speeches and workshops around the world to help leaders master these skills. I'm fond of telling prospective clients that I'm in the "wisdom business." That's why I am excited about this new book and the work that Paul Houston and Stephen Sokolow are doing with their Center for Empowered Leadership. They believe not only in empowered leadership but in empowering leadership based on core principles that touch the humanity of those inside the organization, as well as those outside whom the organization serves.

This book could not have come at a better time. The world is yearning for wise leaders who empower team members and help them succeed faster. I encourage you to not only to read it, but *devour* it, and more important, put these concepts to work until they become new habits for you. What Paul and Steve have to say will help you become a *wise leader* who has mastered the art and science of building positive organizations that consistently achieve extraordinary results and a sustainable competitive advantage *through* people.

Wolf J. Rinke, CSP, PhD is president of Wolf Rinke Associates, Inc., and author of *Winning Management: 6 Fail-Safe Strategies for Building High-Performance Organizations* and *Don't Oil the Squeaky Wheel and 19 Other Contrarian Ways to Improve Your Leadership Effectiveness*, as well as contributor to *Leadership: Helping Others to Succeed*.

Preface

Dr. Paul D. Houston is the former executive director of the American Association of School Administrators, and Dr. Stephen L. Sokolow is a former superintendent of schools who now serves as executive director of the Center for Empowered Leadership. Dr. Houston and Dr. Sokolow each have more than thirty-five years of successful leadership experience in schools and school-related organizations across America. Over the years, both men have become increasingly aware of the spiritual underpinnings of their work as leaders, and the ways in which those underpinnings can lead to wisdom. Whenever they have been together, the conversation inevitably turned to the universal principles that infuse and govern their work as leaders and as human beings.

Dr. Houston and Dr. Sokolow embarked on a journey to discover those spiritual principles that form the basis of enlightened leadership—for example, trust, love, hope, serving others, gratitude, and the role of intention—and to organize them in a way that makes them understandable and accessible to everyone. Enlightened leadership is wise leadership, they concluded, and enlightened leaders are wise leaders. One of the discoveries they made is that we all become wiser leaders by activating and embodying the spiritual principles that already exist within each of us.

Having identified the principles that guide and inform wise leaders, Dr. Houston and Dr. Sokolow formulated a series of probing questions to reveal what they have come to know about these principles. By reflecting on such questions—Why is it important for leaders to be trustworthy? How can leaders foster an attitude of gratitude?—readers will benefit from their own insights as well as the unfolding story shared by Dr. Houston and Dr. Sokolow.

The path to wise leadership is a journey of discovery. It is the journey of discovering who we really are, what our gifts are, and how we can give our gifts to the world. It is the journey of becoming the best version of ourselves and bringing out the best in others. It is the collective journey of bringing out the best that is in the world and of helping the world choose its best and brightest future. The need for wise leadership based upon spiritual principles has never been greater.

We can change the world. In fact, that's what we all do each and every day in ways large and small, intended or not. The authors of this book share a common purpose with you and everyone who is drawn to this book. Put simply, we have a deep and abiding desire to make our world better. We want it to be better for everyone, but especially for our children. The process is already underway because we have unequivocally declared our intention. Now what?

Having an intention is a good place to start, but it is not enough. Our statement of intention declares *what* we want to do. However, for an intention to grow in power it must also include the *why* and the *how*. In other words, why do we want to do what we want to do, and how are we going to go about doing it? The reasons that underlie our intentions truly do matter. And of course, without resulting action we are left only with wishful thinking.

By nature, both of us—Paul and Steve—are incurable optimists. We see possibility and opportunity in the darkest of circumstances. We want to be clear about that because by almost any measure our world is in serious trouble on countless fronts. We want to make our world better because everywhere you look the urgent need for betterment is clearly evident. For us, and for you, making our world better carries both a practical and a moral imperative. As a practical matter, security, safety, health, economic well-being, and the environment affect every one of us residents of planet earth. The moral imperative is that, in an interconnected world, each of us has an obligation to do what we can to ensure that the world we leave our children is as good as or better than the one we inherited. If we don't do our part, then how can we expect others to do theirs? So what's the key to shaping a better world?

In two words, *wise leadership*! Not just better or more effective leadership, but truly wise leadership. In a nutshell, we need to profoundly expand the number of wise leaders in every facet of life, both in our social institutions and private corporations.

In our last book, *The Spiritual Dimension of Leadership*, we wrote about enlightened leadership. We took the position that enlightened leadership means doing the *right things*, in the *right way*, at the *right time*, for the *right reasons*. These are the four R's of enlightened leadership. Enlightened leadership is based on wisdom. Think about the people you know who, for the most part, seem to know what to do, how and when to do it, and do so for just reasons. These are the people we think of as wise. And ethical.

We share a number of core beliefs. We hope that you share them or will come to share them as well—namely:

- All of us have been endowed with an array of spiritual principles that lead to wisdom.
- Having an awareness and consciousness of these spiritual principles activates and empowers them, both internally and externally.

- Expressing and embodying these spiritual principles, in turn, empower us and the people we lead.

In our worldview, we are all spiritual beings living in a sacred world. Just as our DNA contains a coded blueprint for our physical being, there exists within us a type of *spiritual* DNA, which contains the archetypical[1] blueprint for our spiritual potentiality. In other words, universal spiritual principles such as love, trust, truth, hope, kindness, and so forth, exist within us as seeds of potentiality. As is true for all seeds, certain conditions are necessary to enable them to germinate and grow.

Our experiences as we move through life determine which of those seeds will be nurtured and when, as well as their respective rates of growth. Awareness and focused consciousness, or attention, activate and empower the seeds of potentiality that reside within us. These seeds open and grow into archetypical patterns of energy that can empower us and others in our sphere of influence. This process is not automatic; it requires thought and action. We not only must understand and espouse a spiritual principle, but we must also *live* it. The more we can actually embody any given spiritual principle, the more powerful it becomes in its effect, and the wiser we become as leaders.

In this book we will present an overview of eighteen spiritual principles of leadership. They will all be familiar to you. We believe that they will resonate with you. This is because they already exist

---

[1] Carl Jung used the term archetype to describe universal motifs such as father, mother, child, king, hero, trickster, shadow, leader, and so forth, which he believed to be present in the collective unconscious of all human beings. We believe that each archetype has an underlying energy pattern that can not only affect our thoughts and actions, but also serve as a driving force in our lives and the lives of others in our sphere of influence.

within you, in both your conscious and unconscious minds, in varying degrees. By reading this book your attention will foster the growth of these principles within you. As you consciously choose to expand the practice of these principles in the way you lead, you will grow in wisdom and become a wiser leader.

Each of the spiritual principles we present in this book is a seed of wisdom. May all of your seeds flower and bear the fruit of the wise leader. Wise leaders will by definition choose to do the right things, in the right way, at the right time, for the right reasons. As the effects of wise leadership ripple across an interconnected world, we will indeed reap what we sow and create a better world for ourselves and our children.

May we empower our own and each other's paths toward wisdom.

Acknowledgments

Bringing this work to publication has been a synchronistic journey. It is a journey that Paul Houston and I began more than twenty-five years ago when we started swapping books with spiritual and mystical themes at Harvard University's summer seminar for superintendents. In an unplanned, inspired moment during the summer of 2000, Paul asked me if I would like to coauthor a book with him about the integration of spirituality and leadership. During the next few years we collaborated on the spiritual principles of leadership in extensive weekly dialogues. Those dialogues became the foundation for our first book, *The Spiritual Dimension of Leadership* (Corwin, 2006), as well as this book, the first in a trilogy on wise leadership.

With that in mind, first I wish to express my heartfelt thanks to Paul for proffering an invitation that changed the course of my life. We have become close friends and partners in a venture that reaches beyond the horizon. My well of gratitude runs deep with all of the people who have contributed to my life's path.

More than forty years ago Professor Lee Olson first introduced me to the spiritual underpinnings of leadership. He was a role model for what it means to truly live your spiritual values. I am indebted to him for his love and guidance and for being a stellar example of a wise and enlightened leader.

My brother Adam is a mystic and an advanced student of esoteric spiritual teachings from the East. He is the wisest person I know. For many years we have been taking weekly "walk 'n' talks" in nature. He has been my guide, teacher, and executive coach. His wise counsel has been invaluable to my growth as a human being, and his spiritual insights have helped to shape my own.

I am a Reiki master and have been practicing Reiki for almost twenty years. Reiki is a form of energy that promotes healing and spiritual growth. I am indebted to Djuna Wojton, a wonderful human being and Reiki master, who has shared her gift with me and countless others.

Alan S. Fellheimer is my lifelong friend. He'll be embarrassed by this, but he is the smartest person I know. More than forty years ago when I was writing my first book—my doctoral dissertation—Alan taught me the craft of writing. Without his countless hours of tutorials, neither that book nor this one would have seen the light of day.

Dr. Muska Mosston is a deceased friend whose spirit I still carry in my heart. A distinguished educator and author, he was like a second brother to me during the fifteen years when our lives converged. He loved the world of ideas, and he loved to write. As we talked about education and leadership, he continually urged me to write a book. He was the third in my rule of 3s to suggest that I attend Harvard's summer seminar for superintendents. Without Muska, I would not have come to know Paul Houston well, and someone else would be writing this acknowledgment.

Paul and I both extend our deep gratitude to our friend and editor, Bob Cole, who polishes our words until they light up and shine with our intended meaning.

My special thanks go to my wife, Laney, for her steadfast love, devotion, and encouragement to pursue my life's work. And last, I want to thank our sons, Brett and Brian, who have been a continuing source of growth for me and who are the source of many insights incorporated into this work.

With heartfelt gratitude,
Stephen L. Sokolow

We are all the sum of what has touched us, and anything I might do is the result of what others have done for me. There are far too many to mention. I would like to thank my father, who grounded my spiritual beliefs with a sense of grace and generosity. He was the best Christian I have ever known because he got the "word" and made it "flesh." My mother gave me my warrior spirit and the common sense necessary to navigate this temporal plane. The late Richard Green made me see myself as more than my past, and my "Tucson Gang" (Rog, Vee, Jack, Sue, Ross, Suzy, Jesse, and Jackie) has been my family through thick and thin.

A number of spiritual guides have come to me when I needed them—the teachers who were there when the student was ready— and to each and all, I am most grateful. My children—Lisa, Suzanne, and Caroline—taught me that while we are connected to the divine, that connection is played out in the chain of life that we receive and pass on to others; also, they make me laugh. I thank the universe for Sandra, who proved that it all comes in the right time and space and who has encouraged this work, and me, to become all that God intended. I want to express my gratitude to my grandchildren Will, Lucy, and Jade, who constantly remind me that we should all remember to approach life as a child—to be open to mystery and magic, to be optimistic beyond all reason, and to remain playful in the extreme. And finally, for Steve, whose focus and determination have kept this work alive and who has taught me more about spirituality and leadership than he might ever imagine.

Steve and I would both like to thank Jan Chapman, who early in this process took our hundreds of hours of mutual mumbling and made sense of it so that a manuscript could eventually emerge.

Paul D. Houston

Introduction

The Wise Leader is organized into four parts. Each part consists of three to six chapters. There are eighteen chapters in all. Each chapter opens with a brief overview and a short story that illustrates one of the seeds of wise leadership. The content of each chapter is divided into six to twelve subheadings. Each chapter concludes with a brief bulleted inset summarizing the key concepts. The seeds of wise leadership described in this book are universal. Therefore anyone in or aspiring to a leadership role will find this work enlightening and useful, including leaders in both the public and private sectors.

Many of the values, beliefs, and principles that guide and sustain leaders have underlying spiritual roots, which we call seeds of wisdom. The more closely we stay in touch with these seeds of wisdom, the more enlightened (i.e., wise) our leadership becomes, and the more effective we become in leading others to a better future.

Given the complexities of the issues we face as leaders, it sometimes seems as though we need the wisdom of Solomon to determine the right course of action. Where does such rare wisdom come from? It comes from within us! It is the divine spark that guides us as we live our own lives and lead others toward a brighter future. Wise leadership is grounded in spiritual principles; because of this, it brings out the best in us and in others. Wise leaders not only know the right things to do, and how to do things right, but they do them for the right reasons.

The seeds of wise leadership, which are the heart of this book, are available to all of us as leaders, and we increase our effectiveness if we are attuned to them. These archetypal seeds are real, and they are accessible to each and every one of us.

Under the right conditions, seeds are planted and given the proper nutrients, which allows them to grow and fulfill their potential. This book contains countless seeds of wisdom that can resonate with the archetypal seeds that spring from within you. As you place your attention on them, they will grow and flourish. As you set your intention to infuse them into your practice of leadership, they will grow. The more you think about them and talk about them, the stronger they will become. The more you use them, the stronger they will become. The more of them you incorporate into your practice of leadership, the wiser you will become.

Just as a handful of acorns can grow into a cluster of oak trees, which in turn bear more acorns and over time become a forest, so too the seeds of wisdom can grow in you and propagate throughout your organization. As you practice—and ultimately come to embody— more and more seeds of wisdom, you will find yourself increasingly doing the right things, in the right way, at the right time, for the right reasons, and you and the world will be better for it.

Part I

CHAPTER 1

The Wisdom of Our Unique Life Lessons

A worldview to which we subscribe is that this place where we live is "earth school." As in all schools, there are lessons to be learned and skills to be mastered. As human beings, we are given the opportunity to learn our life lessons and to grow—or not to grow. Each of us has an individualized curriculum. As we master each life lesson, new ones present themselves in an ongoing array of challenges and opportunities. Knowing this, the wise leader is ever alert for the lessons that may be embedded in the challenges or obstacles he or she confronts. The wise leader is a reflective practitioner who continually tries to learn, grow, and master each life lesson both personally and professionally.

When Steve's son Brian was in his early teens, a little over twenty years ago, he came home from summer camp with a ring in his newly pierced ear. To say that Steve was angry would be putting it mildly. Prior to that summer, Brian had broached the topic of piercing with his father, who made his views about the subject quite clear. His father told him that it wasn't a good idea for him to put holes in his body and that it wasn't manly. It was something that was okay for girls but not for boys. While away from home, Brian chose to disobey his father and have his ear pierced anyway. To buttress his case, Brian brought a letter from his fellow campmates saying how cool Brian looked with his new earring and how all of his friends had decided to do the same thing. Steve was really angry; he thought about all the things he could do to punish his son.

A friend of Steve's happened to be present when Steve first learned what Brian had done. Steve's friend recounted examples from his own life of his own children having done similar things as they were growing up. He said that he had blown his top and that his anger over what he had seen as a challenge to his parental authority had created a serious breach in his relationship with his children. He told Steve, "Let me tell you a life lesson I learned as a result of what happened between me and my children. You can decide if you want to risk what happened to me or take a different course." He told Steve that in close relationships, certainly with immediate family and very close friends, any given episode or interaction between you and the other person is never as important as the relationship itself. "Always remember," he said, "that the relationship is more important than what the person may have done or failed to do. If you keep that in mind, it will affect the way you choose to deal with whatever happens between you and the other person."

Steve took his friend's advice to heart and chose to learn the life lesson the easy way. He allowed Brian to keep his earring but insisted on some controls over where and when it would be worn.

Using Our Experiences to Grow Personally and Professionally

Sometimes solving a problem requires you to behave in a different way. In effect, to deal appropriately with whatever you are encountering requires that you make a shift, which necessitates growth either professionally or personally. We suggest that when you are encountering difficulty, in addition to trying to solve the problem at hand, ask yourself whether what's happening is, in effect, a message from the universe telling you that it's time for you to grow. People tend to look outside of themselves for explanations as to why things are happening in their lives; they don't necessarily ask themselves the question, "Is there something internally, within *me*, that needs to change?"

There's a common tendency to resist life's lessons instead of accepting or even embracing them. Leaders gain in wisdom when they can do just that, when they can say, "What a great problem I'm facing. Bring it on! Let me fully appreciate the whole thing." When you face your problems from this new perspective, they tend to go away, or shrink and shrivel up. Yet prior to doing that, they seemed almost insurmountable. Sometimes embracing a lesson allows you to learn it fully, and then move past it; if you resist the lesson, you can't get past it because you're standing in opposition to it. There's a wall there that you're trying to overcome. By moving toward the problem rather than away from it, you may find an opening to get through, or even a way around it, and suddenly find yourself standing on the other side.

When you embrace a problem, it is important to recognize that there may be a lesson in it for you. You are the participant, but you're also the observer of whatever is unfolding. In the role of observer, step back—not just to gain perspective, but also to think about what lesson is there for you before embracing it.

Life Experiences Can Promote Our Spiritual Growth

Since this is earth school, everything you experience is a life lesson to promote your spiritual growth. Every obstacle, every stumbling block is, in essence, a steppingstone toward greater growth. It's easy *not* to see things in this way because life's events often hurt or are difficult. Life is far different from school, however. In life, first you have the test and then you have the lesson; in school, on the other hand, the sequence is reversed. Life is a much tougher and more demanding environment because you're always being tested so you can learn, grow, and move past whatever level you're on. The only way you can do that is through facing and overcoming challenges. You rarely grow in easy circumstances. Life is like spiritual isometrics. You have to keep pushing and pulling to build the spiritual muscle you need to move forward.

When things are difficult or they don't feel right or are not going well, ask yourself this question, "What is the spiritual lesson here that I need to pay attention to?" It is helpful to ask yourself that question aloud, as though you are addressing it to the universe, because frequently the lesson is not readily apparent. Often it takes reflection and prayer to gain insight as to exactly what the lesson is— whether you need to open up or loosen up or find a better balance, or be more compassionate, and so forth. The supply of lessons created to assist every one of us in growing spiritually is limitless. The first challenge is to identify and understand the nature of the lesson at hand. When you've done that, you've taken an important step toward mastering that particular lesson. Think of the process as a series of skills you need to acquire and ask yourself, "What skill is it that I need to cultivate in order to meet the particular challenges I am confronting at this moment?"

Problems Are Opportunities in Disguise

One of the attributes of wise leadership is an awareness that all problems have opportunities and possibilities embedded within them. Problems are lessons that can move you forward, sometimes even leading to major life breakthroughs. We subscribe to the notion that no door closes without another one opening. There is a pattern or cycle in life in which what looks like a negative often contains the seeds of something positive because it opens up the next opportunity. *It is the possibility behind the problem that offers hope.* That's why wise leaders cultivate optimism, and why this perspective is so important.

In Paul's personal life, the ending of one relationship opened up the possibility of another, much better relationship coming along, which would not have been possible if the other one had not ended. So what could have been regarded as a sad negative experience (one relationship ending) actually became a prelude to the next possibility. We believe that every problem has *something* within it that can be turned into something positive. Within negative events, there is a kernel of something positive if we look for it, name it as such, and then empower it by giving it energy. It is incumbent upon wise leaders to show people the positive potential inherent in the problems they are confronting.

Our nation will never forget the events of 9/11, one of the most terrible events ever to occur on American soil; yet even within that unimaginable anguish and pain has been the opportunity for bravery, heroism, people coming together, outpourings of generosity, caring, and compassion, and a renewed sense of patriotism and the resolve to defeat international terrorism. Even within this most horrific of problems, the possibility of something positive existed.

Clouds Actually Do Have Silver Linings

While some people believe that behind every silver lining is a dark cloud, we hold the opposite view. From a literal perspective, clouds distribute the water that nourishes all life, and under the right conditions that water produces a rainbow, which from biblical times has served as a symbol of possibility and promise—a silver lining.

When circumstances are cloudy, wise leaders need to ask themselves, "What is the silver lining in this situation?" If you don't ask yourself that question, you may miss discovering a way to take advantage of the cloud. Wise leaders are able to take advantage of clouds and darkness by seeing the light or silver lining that can come from seemingly negative circumstances. They have the proactive ability to create a better day by seizing the negative moment and inverting it. In the same way that valleys help give meaning to mountain heights, negative circumstances can be used to illuminate contrasting positive possibilities. By encouraging people to look for silver linings, wise leaders can help them to become possibility thinkers.

If wise leaders not only look for silver linings themselves, but also encourage the people with whom they work to search for the positives within cloudy events or cloudy circumstances, there will be a positive multiplier effect. People may even see different silver linings in the same cloud. Helping people in your organization to process events in this way will help them grow. Wise leaders can challenge others by asking, "What is the positive opportunity here, the silver lining, and can you find it?" When people are given the opportunity to discuss and explore problems from this perspective, you may be surprised by how often they will actually find a silver lining.

Life Lessons Can Be Learned the Hard Way or the Easy Way

How you respond to life lessons is entirely your choice. You can choose to resist the lesson, which makes it much more difficult; resistance creates friction, friction creates heat, and heat burns. When you resist a lesson, you end up burning yourself. Or you can embrace the lesson, which makes the whole process easier. Embracing the lesson at hand doesn't necessarily mean that it will be easily learned, but it may not take you as long to gain insight and grow. Resistance tends to slow everything down. Our attitude often determines how hard or how easy the lessons are in our lives. Some people have extremely hard lives but are able to march right through their lessons, while others don't face that much difficulty, but whatever difficulty they do have seems to end up being magnified. It's not the lessons themselves as much as our reaction to them that makes things difficult; some people really do make mountains out of molehills. People with a strong sense of faith often find that their lessons are easier, less overwhelming, and less lengthy.

Many people deny things that are happening to them. They fail to see the lesson at hand or simply try to rationalize it away. However, the cosmos is mysteriously constructed in such a way that your lesson will not go away just because you attempt to go away from it. The lesson you need to grow pursues you relentlessly in various guises, and it will escalate until you can no longer ignore it. Lessons are like a physical illness that can be treated fairly easily if you go to the doctor right away and take the prescribed remedy, but if you ignore the symptoms and warning signs, over time the illness becomes more serious. So we all need to ask, "How can I address my challenges at the lowest possible level before they grow, and grow in undesirable ways?"

The Weaknesses within Our Strengths Help Us to Understand Life Lessons

Whatever people do best belies an inherent concomitant weakness in their abilities. For example, someone who is very humanistic will sometimes hesitate in making a tough decision or in doing something that will be hurtful to someone else, even though it should be done for the good of the organization. So that extreme humanity also has the power to make a person overly sensitive. There's a teaching in Taoism that too much emphasis on being pretty makes one ugly. In other words, too much emphasis on anything that is positive reveals the weakness within that same character trait. Someone who's really skilled at making money could end up by being greedy, and so forth.

When people appreciate those things that they excel at, it can create a blind spot within them. They might say, "Don't talk to me about X because I'm really good at X." In your areas of strength, it seems counterintuitive that you might also be weak or vulnerable. The last place you might think to examine when you're having a problem is one of your strengths, and yet that's the place it may be most helpful to explore when identifying and grappling with life lessons. Because this seems to be counterintuitive, it can come as a surprise to learn that people have weaknesses embedded within their strengths, and vice versa. This is a fractal that mirrors the relationship between chaos and order in the universe at large. Chaos theory reveals an ongoing dance between chaos and order where embedded within order are seeds of chaos, and vice versa. Perhaps this relationship is best symbolized by the yin-yang symbol. Within the white yang energy is a small black dot of yin energy; conversely, within the black yin energy is a small white dot of yang energy. The wise leader knows this and looks where others won't.

Each Lesson Mastered Opens a Gateway to the Next Lesson

Yogi Berra observed, "It's not over until it's over." With respect to life lessons, however, it's *never* over, because each lesson leads to the next one. We never exhaust the syllabus for our lives. As Roseanne Rosannadana said, "You know, it's always something; if it's not one thing, it's something else."

Here's an irony for you: the mastery of a life lesson leads to the next one, but so does the *failure* of a life lesson. Either way, there's always another lesson awaiting you. But success at a life lesson means you advance, while failure means you must repeat the same lesson. Repeating it usually means that whatever lesson you're facing is presented to you in a more severe form. It's like retention in third grade in elementary school. If you fail the lesson, instead of being promoted you have to repeat third grade to master it, but this time you have an even tougher teacher. Mastery means you're promoted to the next grade and a new set of lessons.

Life is structured so that every time we reach some level of mastery, another level begins. It's as if the ceiling of one level becomes the floor of the next—much like going from the top class in middle school to the bottom class in high school. This progression repeats itself again and again throughout our lives. Now you see the appropriateness of the term "earth school"!

Embedded in this whole process is the notion of movement. If you master a lesson and reach the next stage, yet do not continue to grow, then you stagnate. There really is no rest for the weary. You are never going to reach a stage where there are no new lessons to confront. The wise leader knows that it doesn't matter how wealthy you are or how healthy you are or how successful you are—the cycle is unending.

Each Ending Creates the Opportunity for a New Beginning

Steve's youngest son went through a divorce. He grieved over the loss of the relationship, but in the end it created the opportunity for him to form a new relationship with someone else—a relationship that was much healthier than the first. This same kind of transformative experience may also happen with the loss of a job and with other endings. As events in our lives come to an end, it seems to create openings for other events to unfold. What we do with those new opportunities is always up to us. We subscribe to the adage that when one door closes, another opens. That's a helpful perspective to have because when things are ending, we may be so focused on the ending, or the loss we are experiencing, that we can fail to recognize the doorway of opportunity that is opening.

Wise leaders help people look at endings with an eye toward recognizing the opportunities for new beginnings; they also help people understand that, as things are beginning, eventually there will be a natural cycle of closure, and this is part of the natural cycle of endings and beginnings in the universe, with each creating the opportunity for the other. Wise leaders understand that cycle, and they lead from that premise. Other leaders don't see change as natural; they are more oriented to the status quo and try to hold on to what they have. The irony, of course, is that you cannot hold on, because the harder you try to hold on to something, the more it slips through your fingers.

To become The Wise Leader:

- Use your professional and personal experiences to grow as a human being.
- Understand that your life experiences create the opportunity for your spiritual growth.
- See problems as opportunities in disguise.
- Discover the silver linings in the clouds of life.
- Strive to master life lessons in their easiest form.
- Know that the weaknesses within your own strengths hold a key to understanding some of your life lessons.
- Understand that each lesson mastered opens the gateway to the next lesson.
- Understand that each ending creates the opportunity for a new beginning.

CHAPTER 2

The Wisdom of Revering All Living Beings

We have a fundamental respect for all life, but especially for human beings who, according to the Bible, are made in the image of God. In this chapter, among other things, we will talk about the three D's—diversity, dignity, and divinity—and how they relate to wise leadership. Life is our most precious gift, a gift worthy of our deepest appreciation and reverence.

Many years ago, at a national conference of the American Association of School Administrators in Atlantic City, New Jersey, Steve stopped in the men's room of one of the casinos. To his surprise, a shoeshine stand was set up in the men's room. All of the chairs were empty. On the spur of the moment Steve decided his shoes could use a shine. An elderly Asian man smiled and began shining his shoes. This man went about his work with a deliberateness and dedication that caught Steve's attention. Steve watched the man apply coat after coat of polish and then rub and brush each coat with great care. Long after Steve thought his shoes looked good, the man kept polishing and refining his handiwork. Steve's shoes started to shine with a brilliance that was greater than the day they were brand new.

"No one has ever shined my shoes like that," Steve said aloud. The man smiled and said, "When you leave here, some of me is in your shoes." Steve thought to himself, "This is like a scene from a movie, where an angel appears in human form to teach you something." In that moment Steve felt like the student in the presence of a wise teacher. Here was a person who was doing a menial task, but he was giving it everything he had, and somehow he created a sparkle and deep beauty that hadn't been there before. It was apparent that this man took enormous pride in his work. Steve looked at the man with reverence, and the man appeared to sparkle somehow, radiating an inner peace and beauty. From that experience Steve learned that it doesn't matter what our station in life is or what we do; rather it is *how* we do what we do, and how much of who we are that we put into what we do, that really matters. When we give our all, we make a lasting connection that has the power to truly affect others.

Valuing Diversity Demonstrates a Reverence for All Beings

It's easiest to love yourself. It's harder to love other people, and it's hardest of all to love people who are different from us. The issue of diversity in our society, or any society, is a difficult one—actually, our society handles diversity better than most. You have to ask, "How big is your circle going to be? How inclusive can you be with people who are different?" To the extent that you fail to open up your circle, you also fail to reach a broader view of things. Without seeing diversity as a positive, it's difficult to be a wise leader. In many ways, diversity is an opportunity to learn how to love. It's pretty easy to love people who are like you. The less like you they are, the more difficult it is to be open to their differences, and often we have a hard time being open and loving to those who are different.

We believe that there is a divine spark in everyone. If you share this belief, then that belief becomes the basis for the way you behave toward other people, including those who are different, for how can you behave toward that which reflects the divine in any way other than with a sense of reverence?

We believe that there's a payoff for this spiritual perspective. As a wise leader who views all people as having divine gifts and as being on their own paths toward growth and personal evolution, you can play an important role in that process by the way you view and treat others. When you support and value people regardless of their ethnic or cultural background, they feel a sense of gratitude and want to do more rather than less for you and for the organization of which you are a part. The wise leader knows that the effect of such feelings is to enhance organizational productivity, creativity, and capacity.

Increasing Our Awareness of the Divine in Others

First, it is necessary to arrive at an awareness of the divine in ourselves. Once you have a deep understanding of the wellsprings of the divine within yourself, then you can see that this same divinity is true for other human beings. Having a sense of the divine in others can assist you when you move outside of the church, synagogue, or mosque, in coming to realize that people do not give up their spark of divinity when they move from one venue to another. If you accept that there is a spark of divinity in all beings, then what are the implications of that acceptance in terms of how you treat others?

There was a well-known prisoner of war during the Vietnam era, a navy pilot who was released from captivity after four or five years. Several years later, when he was attending a reunion of the veterans who had served on his ship, a man approached him and said, "I'm so glad to see you alive and well."

The pilot said, "I'm sorry, but I don't remember you."

The seaman responded, "No, I'm sure that you don't remember me. I was just a navy seaman second class. You were a flier, so our paths didn't really cross, but I was so pleased to hear that when your plane went down you were able to get out of it and land safely and, even though you were captured and taken prisoner, that you were still alive."

The flier replied, "But I don't understand why it's so important to you."

The seaman said, "Well, I packed your chute."

Think about this: Who's packing *your* chute? The support people in organizations such as custodians, assistants, and secretaries are the people who pack your chute. As the boss, you may have the glory job. You're out there flying, but if you go down in flames, you better hope that somebody packed your chute and that he did a good job of it. Whose chute are *you* packing?

Treating Everyone with Dignity and Respect

How do you want to be treated? That's a relevant question because whatever you give out, you're going to get back in one form or another. At a basic level, you treat people with dignity and respect because otherwise you have no right to expect anything more for yourself. Another reason is profound yet simple: they are all God's children. You didn't make them. They were created by a higher

17

being and therefore deserve to be treated accordingly. Conversely, when you fail to treat everyone with dignity and respect, in effect you're being disrespectful toward the divine. People may realize they are not showing respect to another person, but rarely do they think of that other person as an extension of the divine.

As a minister's son, Paul was raised in a church setting that allowed him ample opportunity to observe others. He saw people on Sunday, and then he saw what they did all week. It always disturbed him to see people who professed to be holy treat other people poorly. He thought to himself, "I don't think those two things match up." He observed an inherent conflict between professing a certain level of religious fervor and holy thought and then turning around and treating your fellow humans poorly, gossiping about them, saying hurtful things, or creating harmful situations. That dichotomy has always bothered him. He felt a person should actually *live* his spiritual values and try to demonstrate the same kind of fervor on Monday that he displayed on Sunday.

It's difficult for people to live up to their own expressed values, and it's something that everyone has to work on, including us. The wise leader knows it's helpful to seek feedback from others as to how you are doing because it's pretty easy to fall off the wagon and not operate in ways that you espouse and to which you ostensibly aspire.

Wise Leaders Listen More and Talk Less

Yogi Berra once said, "You can observe a lot just by watching." The corollary is that you can hear a lot just by listening. Most of the time, when people talk, they tend to be pretty self-centered and focused on themselves. They pontificate to someone else, putting themselves above the other person and saying, in essence, "I'm hot stuff, I've got something wonderful to share, and I'm going to share it with you." Now it's true that in many cases you can help others by offering advice or providing insight or inspiration. It's necessary, though, to get beyond your ego. Listening—real listening—as opposed to just cocking your ear at somebody—is *active* listening, where you're trying not only to hear what others are saying, but also to understand and empathize with it. At that point you are being "other-directed." By really listening to the other person you are acknowledging his value, and that's different from talking at him.

If you are a good listener, and listen more than you talk, people notice and appreciate it. Other people, in turn, become more willing to listen to you because you have modeled what it means to be a good listener. They would like to listen to you as attentively as you've listened to them. This dynamic provides the opportunity for real collaboration, and for some sense of communion or community among people. Active listening may actually strengthen the energy connection that is occurring in a dynamic exchange between people. The wise leader knows that *active listening has power*. It is evocative. It creates the conditions that allow another person's thoughts and feelings to come to the surface and be expressed.

Wise Leaders Don't Assume They Know Another's Point of View

When you make an assumption, you're unconsciously declaring that you know more than the other person because you're a step ahead of him. You're saying, "I don't need to pay any more attention to you." You've already jumped to the chase, when in fact you may have jumped to the wrong place. Making hasty assumptions is even disrespectful, because you haven't given the other person his moment to share something. Consider how aggravating it is to be in a discussion with someone who interrupts you and argues back before you've finished saying your piece. Outraged, you think, "Let me finish!" So often where you're going with your argument is not what they're answering. People often make assumptions that are dead wrong because they haven't paid attention to what the other person is saying.

When you don't assume another person's point of view, often he will surprise you. If you take the extra time to say to a person, "Tell me what this looks like through your eyes," he will tell the story from his perspective; very often it's not what you were expecting. You may be partially correct, but you may not have the right flavor or the right context. Steve is an insightful guy, and yet people frequently have a particular take on something or a viewpoint that's not quite what he thought it would be. He has found that the more he asks, the more he learns. People are usually willing to tell you what they think, especially if you ask them directly. Even if you disagree with someone's perspective, the fact that you've taken the time to understand it seems to develop an appreciation in the other person that at least he was heard. If you've come to a different position, he knows that you've taken his views into consideration and is better able to accept your decision.

In Resolving Disputes, Wise Leaders Seek to Preserve the Dignity of Adversaries

Paul recalls being caught in a negative situation involving an adversary and the challenge of trying to treat him with a sense of divinity when he seemed like such a devil. Paul thought, "If I treat him like a devil, I've lowered myself in the process. If I can treat him as one of God's children, despite how mistaken and misguided he seems, at least I'm not lowering my own energy and my own dignity to a different level."

An important part of the issue of the dignity of others is your own dignity. To the degree that you are unwilling to preserve the dignity of your adversary, you're also failing to preserve your own dignity. If you want to preserve your own dignity, you need to preserve that of others as well.

Another argument for treating people with dignity is a variation of the Golden Rule. If you don't treat your adversaries with dignity, you're giving them license not to treat you with dignity. Your adversaries, in general, are people with whom you're going to have a continuing relationship; you want to keep that relationship on as high a plane as possible. One way of doing that is according adversaries a level of dignity and respect, saying, for example, "Let's agree to disagree," or "We're not on the same wavelength on this issue." The wise leader tries to take conflict out of the personal realm and keep it focused on the issues and on particular priorities or values. The wise leader knows that the way to preserve (or even enhance) the dignity of adversaries is not to sink to attacking the person, because you're potentially attacking that inner core that we hold to be divine.

Striving to Find Common Ground Can Be a Way of Demonstrating Reverence toward Others

The search for common ground is an effort at peace-making. It is finding shared space with someone else. It is acknowledging that, to some degree, you are in the same boat together whether you want to be or not. And it is looking for points of overlap and points of connection, as opposed to focusing on points of difference and dissonance.

The search for common ground is really an attempt to find a place of communion. It is also a proactive process of looking for it, because what you are acknowledging is, "I don't like your positions very much. We don't agree on much; we're really in different places. Having said that, here are some places where we can stand together because I think we probably line up on this one, so let's accentuate the positives, eliminate the negatives, and don't mess with Mr. In-Between." Basically, that's what you're doing when you work to create common ground. You are accentuating areas of common purpose and playing down existing differences. Your aim is to find a place to stand with the other person, which also demonstrates a level of reverence.

Finally, by your words and actions you are saying, "Deep down at everyone's core there is goodness, and this inherent goodness is capable of creating common ground even if there doesn't appear to be any." The wise leader knows that the dignity with which you treat the other person, and his respect for your dignity, provide a necessary foundation. We owe it to ourselves, and to the people we represent and serve, to find or even create common ground, though that process can be elusive and difficult.

To become The Wise Leader:

- Value diversity.
- See the divine in others.
- Treat everyone with dignity and respect.
- Listen more and talk less.
- Don't assume you know another's point of view.
- In resolving disputes, seek to preserve the dignity of adversaries.
- Strive to find common ground.

CHAPTER 3

The Wisdom of Focusing on the Positive

Focusing on the positive is an indispensable principle of wise leadership. Being positive engenders hope, but it does much more than that—it is a force that helps create the positive possibilities you envision. Belief helps shape reality, and focusing on the positive helps shape a *positive* reality. In a dualistic world, where the positive and negative scales seem roughly in balance, a positive focus can shift the balance in your favor.

When Paul's daughters were young children, he recalls hearing a story about a little boy named Peter practicing baseball in the backyard. The boy's mother and father were watching him play. Peter tossed the ball up in the air, swung his bat, missed, and said, "Strike one." He grabbed the ball, looked it over, pitched it up, swung his bat, missed, and again yelled, "Strike two!" Once again, he picked up the ball, threw it up, swung and missed, and shouted, "Strike three!" The father walked over to where his son was standing and said, "Son, aren't you a little tired of this? Wouldn't you like to play catch instead?" Peter looked at him and said, "What, quit now when I'm pitching a no-hitter?" While this story is probably apocryphal, it brings home the point that things are often a matter of perspective.

One person's negative experience can be another person's positive experience, depending on how he chooses to look at whatever he is experiencing.

Focus on the Positive

Wise leaders focus on the positive possibilities inherent in virtually all circumstances. Some leaders turn lights on, and other leaders turn lights off; the only way you can present light and possibility to people is to be a possibility thinker yourself.

Wise leaders have to be the most positive people in their organization because they have to lift everyone else up, and sometimes that's not easy to do. During the dark days following 9/11, horrible as it was, Mayor Rudolph Giuliani kept focusing people on their future, telling them that New York City would come back, that in the end the city would be okay, and that citizens should use this tragedy as an opportunity to come together. He turned an extreme negative into a positive possibility. During England's most challenging days in World War II, Winston Churchill did the same thing for his countrymen. And Franklin Roosevelt bolstered America's spirits in difficult times when he told the American people, "The only thing we have to fear is fear itself." Wise leaders help people rise to their highest place and seek their highest purpose by presenting them with positive possibilities.

Leaders influence the way others see the events in their own lives. The dynamic is the same as when a little child falls down and looks at his mother or father to see if he's okay or not. If the mother or father has a reassuring look that communicates a positive message, then the child believes that things are all right. If the parent looks fearful, then the child gets the message that things are *not* okay. People in an organization are always looking to the leader to see if things are okay. Whether people are aware of it or not, they look to their leader for cues as to how they should feel or react. If leaders want the people in their organization to see things in a positive light, those leaders have to model it, and wise leaders do just that.

Being Positive Is Contagious

Being positive is contagious, but so is being negative. If you are in a leadership position, what are you choosing to spread? Are you going to be Susie Sunshine or Typhoid Mary? You don't even have to be in a leadership position for these attitudes to be contagious. Whatever leaders do is magnified, but you also see peers in organizations who affect others in very positive ways. They seem to lift up everyone around them. On the other hand, other people (including many leaders, unfortunately) are very negative and tend to bring others down.

Positive and negative attitudes function like emotions, and emotions are contagious. When we're around people who are feeling sad, we human beings tend to pick up on that sadness and feel sadness ourselves. Or if we're part of a group and someone starts laughing, the next thing you know, the number of laughing people increases. There's something about expressing emotions in the presence of others that strikes a sympathetic chord. This doesn't happen as often when people make an effort to "put on a happy face," because people can usually discern whether or not feelings are genuine. When feelings are indeed genuine, others often automatically tune in to them.

Genuine positive feelings manifest themselves in much the same way—much like transmitting an energy vibration that everyone else has a receiver for, or like being a member of an orchestra and tuning your instrument to the first violin. People seem to have an internal emotional tuning fork. In the case of an orchestra, the process is conscious and ritualized, whereas when people feel their positive or negative feelings rise or fall in accordance with those of their leaders, the process is largely unconscious. Knowing this, the wise leader exudes a positive demeanor.

Being Positive Serves to Reassure Others

While playing, young children often look to their parents for reassurance when venturing into unknown territory. They want to know if it is safe to proceed. Adults are no different. At some level, people are always checking the universe and asking, "Is it okay? Is it safe out there? Can I go outside now?" The positive voice inside you says, "Go ahead; it's safe," while your negative voice sends discouraging messages. When leaders decide it's okay to "go out and play," meaning to venture into the unknown, others follow them out onto the field of play. When leaders are relaxed enough to be playful, even in stressful situations, others find such behavior reassuring.

The notion of playfulness can be useful in this context because positive energy and positive thinking encourage playfulness, and playfulness releases and engenders creativity. Conversely, playfulness releases positive energy, and it is also a gateway to laughter. Laughter releases chemicals in your body that make you healthier and even fight disease, as Norman Cousins fought his cancer by looking at funny movies and laughing all day. He brought his cancer to a standstill, reaping the effects of the positive energy that he had created. So the notion of being in a positive space, according to what the medical profession is now telling us, is physically as well as mentally healthier. And if it's physically healthier, it's probably also organizationally healthier. Wise leaders turn positive energy loose in their organizations and, in so doing, make their organizations healthier for the people in them. Healthy environments engender feelings of safety and well-being, which people find reassuring.

Being Positive Helps Yield Positive Results

The concept of a self-fulfilling prophecy posits that if you believe something, it increases the likelihood that you'll actually help to create that reality. That's true both positively and negatively, of course, but since most people prefer positive results to negative results, they would choose to invest their thinking in the positive possibility.

The awareness that being positive helps yield positive results also stems from the notion that like begets like. Whatever you sow, you will reap. Whatever you send out, you get back. Wise leaders tend to focus on the positive possibilities that they envision. They use every opportunity to express those positive views in many ways, including writing, speaking, visual imagery, symbols, and even slogans or songs. The more approaches used by leaders, the more likely it becomes that those results will manifest as reality. Being positive increases the likelihood of a positive outcome.

Realistically, because it's not possible to control everything, people who think positively are still going to experience some negative outcomes. Nonetheless, we feel that you increase your odds dramatically by being positive, by being trusting, by investing your energies in the positive side of the equation. People who try to control the world find that the world is ultimately uncontrollable. We understand that generally you're not going to be able to control events and realize everything that you might wish to see happen, but those leaders who seem to be the most successful are the ones who emit positive thought patterns—and somehow the universe seems to support them.

Positive Consciousness Creates Positive Reality

Positive consciousness has to do with thinking and attitude. Wise leaders, in the privacy of their own thoughts, try to display a positive orientation regardless of the issue. All of us really do have a large measure of control over how we use our thought-energy to increase the likelihood of positive outcomes, regarding what unfolds in the world. Most people think that their thoughts are merely an internal processing mechanism that has no impact on the world until action is taken. For the most part, people are not aware that their thoughts have power in terms of the consciousness that is projected.

The Bible tells us, "As a man thinks, so shall he be." One interpretation of this adage is that our thoughts become behaviors, and our behaviors become reality. A related quote from Lao Tzu says, "Watch your thoughts; they become words. Watch your words; they become actions; Watch your actions; they become habit; Watch your habits; they become character. Watch your character; it becomes your destiny." Following that line of thinking, positive thoughts have the power to create the reality of positive character. But we believe that positive thoughts can do even more than that. Positive thoughts have an infectious quality that spreads to others around us, and beyond. Positive thoughts also attract like-minded people, who can then support one another in creating the positive reality that they envision.

It's pretty hard, if not impossible, to create a positive reality without a positive consciousness. The process of creating a positive reality is a sequential one; one step leads to the next, creating a path. The path ultimately determines where your journey takes you. As a wise leader, if you want your journey to take you to a positive reality, you have to start with positive thoughts and a positive attitude in terms of the way you choose to see the world.

Being Positive Serves as a Powerful Motivating Force

When you are being positive, you see the possibilities and the potential in the people with whom you work. People appreciate the fact that you believe in them and that you see them in a positive light. Don't all of us really want to be thought of in a positive way? When leaders think highly of you, don't you want to act in a way that justifies their view of you?

Some believe that motivation arises internally. If that is so, then the task for wise leaders becomes creating the conditions to unwrap it. How do you free people's positive inherent goodness? We think it's freed by believing in people, by giving them a safe place to fall, so they know that when they try, the price of failure is not so great that they wouldn't want to get up and try again. Everyone needs a sense of safety, a sense of belief, and a sense of purpose; people understand the power of working toward a goal that makes them want to achieve something.

Before the beginning of the 2009-10 basketball season, one college coach taped to the locker of every one of his players a picture of the stadium in Indianapolis that would be the site of the NCAA Final Four tournament. He wrote a note on the photo that said, "What have you done today that will help you get here?" What a motivational tool! He didn't say, "This is what you have to do today to get here." He asked his players the question, "What have you done today that will help you get here?" Each player probably answered that question in a different way. The subtext of the coach's message was, "I believe you're capable of being here at the end of this year. I've assessed your abilities, and I feel that this possibility is within our grasp." At the end of the season, that team played in the Final Four.

Positive People Are Inspired (in Spirit)

We think it's easier to be positive if you're inspired or, as Wayne Dyer puts it, "in spirit." Paul has a close friend who is remarkably positive despite having endured some extremely difficult events in her life—losing two husbands, an unhappy marriage, and so forth. He asked her, "How do you do that? Where does it come from?" She replied that a lot of her positive attitude has to do with her spiritual beliefs; somehow she found inspiration that led her to a positive place. Paul has always considered himself to be a generally positive person, even when he was less spiritual than the person he has become. As he's become more spiritual, however, he has found that it's even easier for him to be positive. If you see the world as essentially neutral, you can be positive about it—that is, you can have a sense of optimism and possibility without thinking there's necessarily anything at work except your own behavior. But the notion of being "in spirit" makes life much lighter and easier because you believe that you have help. You do not have to carry the load by yourself because you have another, greater force carrying the load *with* you.

Paul may have been positive in his early years without being in touch with why or where his attitude sprang from. He now believes that a good part of his positive attitude grew out of his inner connection with the divine, even though he was not aware of it at the time.

From our exploration, both separately and together, we've come to believe that there is a profound correlation between inspiration and being positive. Put simply, the more inspired you are, the more positive you become. Moreover, it may even be that being positive actually has its roots in being divinely inspired, either consciously or unconsciously. Wise leaders are inspired.

We Should Surround Ourselves with Positive People

Positive people contribute their positive energy to those around them. This is a perfect example of what people mean when they use the phrase "win-win." When you're involved with positive people, everybody gains; you gain, they gain, and those in their immediate circle gain. Leaders who are torchbearers of light are going to attract negative forces because opposites attract, but that's not by choice. As a wise leader, however, when you have a choice in selecting people, you can opt for those who have a positive orientation.

Over the years, as a superintendent of schools, Steve had the opportunity to select hundreds of people for employment. One of the things he looked for—either overtly or at a subtle level—was a positive orientation that was reflected in the candidate's attitude and background. He sought positive people. Steve used to ask people to describe their ideal boss, and the qualities of their ideal coworkers. He was trying to get a sense of the kind of people to whom prospective staff members would be attracted. Enthusiasm, for instance, is one indication of a positive orientation. He asked people such questions as: "What excites you professionally? What are you enthusiastic about? What are you proud of? What types of people do you want to spend time with? What type of supervisor are you hoping to work for?" Questions such as these provide some valuable insights into whether or not prospective employees tend to have a positive orientation.

While we recognize that there are times when even cynics can play an important role in providing balance in an organization, we think that, over time, organizations are best served by having a preponderance of positive people.

To become The Wise leader:

- Focus on the positive.
- Know that being positive is contagious.
- Know that being positive is reassuring to others.
- Know that being positive yields positive results.
- Know that having a positive consciousness creates a positive reality.
- Know that negative thought patterns can be transformed into positive ones.
- Know that being positive is a powerful motivating force.
- See positive people as being inspired.
- Surround yourself with positive people.

CHAPTER 4

The Wisdom of Trust

Trust is a fundamental principle of wise leadership. It may well be the foundation upon which everything else is built. We all want to be trusted. We all want to be trustworthy because it not only says something about who we are, it also says something about the way others see us. Trust is an empowering force.

When Paul was superintendent in Tucson, Arizona, the district's mainframe computer was dying. At that time Tucson was a manufacturing center for a major company that sold mainframe computers. The company had pretty well convinced the school board to purchase a new mainframe for several million dollars. A member of Paul's senior staff told him that one of the district's young technology assistants would like to talk to him before he made his decision about the new mainframe. The senior staffer seemed impressed with the young man, so Paul agreed to meet with him.

When the young man met Paul, he asked, "Do you have a boat?"

Paul said, "No, why are you asking me about a boat? I thought we were going to talk about computers."

The technology assistant replied, "Well, with that computer you're getting ready to buy, if you had a boat, at least you could use it for an anchor."

Paul responded, "You're telling me that we're getting ready to make a mistake?"

The young man said, "Oh, absolutely—a three-million-dollar mistake!"

"So what would be a better option?" Paul asked.

The immediate response: "Distributed networking."

At that time few people had even heard of distributed networking. The young man continued, "I've heard some of your speeches. You talk about education being a loosely coupled system, and you want more power to be given to the schools. Why would you have technology that centralizes all the power when you are trying to achieve something very different?"

As the conversation continued, Paul realized that what the young man was saying made a lot more sense than what the Tucson district was preparing to do. Paul went back to his cabinet to talk about distributed networking. All his senior administrators thought he'd lost his mind. The computer company put pressure on the school board to block the networking plan, but Paul resisted. The young man had no status within the district, but there was something in his innocence in just wanting to do the right thing that trumped everyone else's agenda.

The outcome was that Paul put his faith in his young assistant and successfully won approval to install the distributed networking system district-wide. Within a year, major companies were coming to Tucson to see the new system in operation. Tucson leaped from being five years behind the technology curve to five years ahead of it—all based on a single decision that was grounded in Paul's trust in another person's judgment. It was one of those great risks a leader takes because of trust in another person—and it turned out to be trust well placed.

Why It Is Important for Leaders to Be Trusting

With respect to wise leadership, there is nothing more important than being trusting. It's hard to be positive if you're not trusting. It's hard to have reverence if you're not trusting. Being trusting is the *first* thing you have to be. It implies a sense of openness, of possibility, of acceptance, of detachment. The doorway to many spiritual principles of leadership opens through being trusting. We believe that trust is where you must start because it's like the first floor of a building. You get on the elevator of a high-rise building starting at the first floor. Being trusting is the first floor of wise leadership; it opens the doorway to everything else.

If you can't trust, it will be difficult to embody other spiritual principles of leadership. Our experience has shown us how little trust there is in many organizations. When we talk with people in leadership positions, we often find a lack of trust and a strong, almost rigid belief that things must be done in certain ways because "you really can't trust people." This view says that you must guard against other people, protect yourself, and create boundaries and walls because without them you can't possibly succeed. Beware, though: every wall you build is a wall against trust. Every door you close and lock is a door that shuts out trust. If you want to break through walls and open doors, the place to start is with trust.

Trust is the recognition of the divine in someone else. *If you believe as we do that everyone has a divine spark, a good place to start is to trust that it's there.* Related to that divine spark is a sense of the innate goodness in people. We have found that being trusting is one of the conditions that nurtures and unlocks people's innate goodness and divinity. Wise leaders understand that trust is a spiritual force that truly empowers other people and brings out the best in them.

Why It Is Essential for Leaders to Be Trustworthy

Acting in a trustworthy manner encourages others to behave in the same way. If you're not trustworthy yourself, you won't be able to provide the impetus for other people to behave in that manner. In organizations (or in any interactions among human beings), there is a spiral—an interplay—where whatever one person starts the other responds to. When one person begins an interaction in a negative way, then the response will be negative. If someone starts in a positive way, the response tends to be positive. Therefore, if you're looking for trustworthiness in others, you need to start by being trustworthy yourself. Whatever you sow, you'll reap. If you want trust, not only must you be trusting, you must also be trustworthy.

Integrity and trustworthiness are inextricably linked. If you are trustworthy, you live your integrity. People can rely on your word, people can rely on your commitments, and people can rely on your goodwill in seeking to do things that will benefit them, or at the very least not be harmful to them.

Let's think about the word "integrity." At its core, integrity is a sense of being integrated. When you are integrated, all of the pieces fit. When you're dealing with someone whom you don't trust, something doesn't fit properly. Something seems out of synch. When you're dealing with someone you don't feel you can trust, even though there may be a large percentage of what they say and do that makes sense, there is something that doesn't quite match. This is different from the way you feel about someone whom you trust. Everything seems to fit. Integrity and trustworthiness are entwined because both require a fit between your words and actions. They also require a fit between your words and your affect. When people's words and their affect do not match, others can feel that they are putting on a false face and are not trustworthy. Wise leadership becomes difficult—maybe even impossible.

Why It Is Important to Trust Yourself

It is important to trust yourself because you can't do anything for someone else that you can't do for yourself first. Our ability to give *anything*—whether it is love or trust or something else—starts with our ability to have it to give. There's absolutely no way to create a trusting environment with other people if you don't have a high degree of trust in yourself. Now the follow-up question: How do you learn to trust yourself?

If, upon reflection, you realize that you don't trust yourself, it might be useful to reflect on your life experiences to identify those factors or experiences that have caused you not to trust yourself. Perhaps you don't trust yourself because, in fact, you really haven't been trustworthy. It's very difficult to learn to trust yourself without first gaining some insight as to why you don't. For example, someone who has tried a lot of things and failed may not trust himself because of that poor track record. From a spiritual perspective, perhaps such a person simply hasn't been looking in the right places within himself. He may have to search within by meditating, or through some other introspective process, to get in touch with who he really is. Or maybe his feeling of self-mistrust arises because he's operating in a way that's inconsistent with who he really is, but he doesn't realize it. Since it can be difficult to see yourself clearly, talking with a trusted friend or even some counseling sessions may help you gain insight into why or under what circumstances you don't feel that you can trust yourself.

Trust is a feeling as well as a choice, and you can only modify behaviors that are counterproductive in terms of trusting yourself if you have some understanding as to where those feelings come from. Trusting yourself is essential to wise leadership because it also engenders trust in others.

Learning to Trust Your Higher Self

We encourage you to recognize, or at least be open to the idea, that you have a higher self. Your higher self, sometimes called your soul or divine spark, is available to you for guidance. The higher self is a fount of wisdom available to each of us, once we learn how to access it. Through our higher self we receive guidance from the universe, either internally or externally or both. The higher self is the divine aspect of who we are. It is our connection to the divine, which means that every one of us has access to divine wisdom. And if you can't trust divine wisdom, what can you trust?

There are many ways of seeking divine guidance. One is by simply asking for it from your higher self. Just as there are many ways of seeking divine guidance, the guidance you receive may take many forms. Sometimes you may get a strong feeling that something is right or not right for you. Sometimes you may receive flashes of intuition, or messages in a dream state, or in a meditative state, or when practicing a religious ritual. And sometimes you may receive guidance through other people or synchronistic events. It's not always easy to know when you are receiving the guidance you seek. It may come at surprising times and in surprising ways: in a book or article that you're reading or in a movie you're watching, or from a friend or even a stranger. Once you ask for guidance, you need to be alert to what comes to you, and you need to trust (there's that word again!) that you will receive it.

The hardest part is recognizing the guidance; sometimes it is subtle, and sometimes you may think you're receiving conflicting guidance from different sources. We are not advocates of blind trust. To the extent possible, you should verify and reality-test what you believe is the divine guidance you are receiving. Take it for a test drive, check it out, see if it feels right, and see if it's working. If it is not working, then you may be misreading the advice or misapplying it or assuming that something is coming from a divine source when it is not.

Wise Leaders Must Learn to Trust the Universe

In the context of this book, we use the words universe and *divine* interchangeably. You should learn to trust the universe because the universe is, by definition, always right. It is bigger than you are. It is more powerful than you are. It has been around longer, and it knows a lot more. When you come to a point that you can trust the workings of the universe, then you align yourself with a power much greater than yourself.

We trust the universe. We know people who don't trust it at all, and even believe that there's nothing there to trust. Most of us would place ourselves somewhere along that continuum between absolute trust in the universe and total lack in trust or even disbelief. We suggest that you look back at the way events have played out in different aspects of your life. By looking backward, you may be able to see some of the patterns that have created opportunities for your growth, the lessons you have learned, and opportunities to use your innate gifts. Look backward and see what has happened in your life. Maybe things that you didn't think would be good for you turned out to be very good. At the time, you didn't think it was good: the job you didn't get, the house you wanted to buy but lost to someone else, the relationship that failed. At the time you wouldn't have made those choices for yourself, and yet, looking backward, you can see that these events turned out to be positive factors in your life. We are not saying that many such crossroads were not difficult or stressful or painful—only that, ultimately, they proved to be good for you, helping you become the person you are today. Realizing that such patterns and processes are still unfolding in your life may help you join the ranks of those of us who trust the universe.

Give Trust as a Gift Whenever Possible

One of the most precious gifts people can give others is their trust. Some leaders say, "I'll give you trust when you earn it." The reality is that there simply isn't enough time for everyone to earn your trust. But you can give trust anyway, as a gift. What greater gift is there than the gift of trust? Trust is nearly priceless.

Suppose someone comes to you seeking permission to do something and you say, "I don't need all the details. I trust you. Just do it. Take care of it." The person looks at you with an expression that asks, "You do?" He wants to see if you really mean it. And you say, "Yes, I do. I trust you." In that exquisite moment, he has a palpable, almost transformative reaction.

What does it mean when we say, "Give trust as a gift"? What are the implications of that gift? For you? For the other person? Obviously, things may go well or not. You may trust someone to handle matters in your absence, and that person may not do the job as well as you had hoped he would. Or he might really mess up! How you respond to that outcome demonstrates what you meant when you said, "I'll trust you."

As a leader, do you mean what you say or not? Do you just say you give your trust and then, if the person falls short, berate him? And does that kind of reaction from you show that you didn't really trust them after all? Or do you come back and say, "I trust you, but I understand that sometimes things don't work out quite the way we had planned or hoped, so let's figure out what we can learn from this. But I want you to know that I still have faith in you, and I still trust you."

Wise leaders know that trust is not a simple act; it's not complete simply because it's bestowed. Trust is an iterative, interactive process that builds through continual reflection and growth. It is an ongoing process in which you continually demonstrate that your trust is true.

To become The Wise Leader:

- **Be trustworthy.**
- **Trust yourself.**
- **Be trusting.**
- **Trust your higher self.**
- **Trust the universe.**
- **Give trust as a gift.**

CHAPTER 5

The Wisdom of Walking the Talk

Wise leaders have integrity—an integrity that comes from within. Their integrity is a manifestation of who they truly are. These are leaders who say what they mean and do what they say. These are leaders whose deeds match their words—their walk is aligned with their talk. That's why people trust them and respond to their leadership. These leaders are authentic. They are who they are. What you see is what you get. Their integrity and authenticity engender trust and serve as a role model for all of us. Wise leaders know the importance of walking their talk; they know that their actions speak louder than their words. Because they live in the spotlight, they are keenly aware that people are always watching what they do and listening to what they say—especially children, who are keen observers of the world around them.

Paul started teaching in North Carolina in the 1960s, right after schools were racially integrated. Suddenly a lot of teachers were teaching children of another race, many for the very first time. Paul remembers a white teacher struggling one day in a class that had many over-aged (for their grade) African American kids. She was telling the students, "I don't know why you don't feel better about this class, why you don't feel good about me. You know I really love you oh-so much."

One of the children said, "Well, if you love me so much, why don't you tell your face?" That little boy knew that something didn't quite match up between this teacher's face and her words. She wasn't being authentic, and that student knew it.

Children (and animals, too) seem to be better than many adults at spotting people who aren't walking their talk or who show an inconsistency between what they espouse and what they do. As a leader, if you can't walk your talk and be what you espouse, the disparity becomes increasingly apparent over time.

Why It Is Important to Walk Your Talk

Authenticity and integrity are essential keys to wise leadership. People recognize these traits from all sorts of subtle messages. Lack of confidence in a leader tends to revolve around the disconnect between what people see and what they hear. So when you're not walking your talk, you're really sending a signal to people that it doesn't matter what you say because what you do speaks much louder—and what you do invalidates everything you've just said. Once you've invalidated what you've said, why should anyone pay attention to anything you're doing or saying?

This dynamic actually springs from our childhood, when we are busy observing the world, and observing our parents even more closely. How often have you heard parents (and teachers) say, "Why don't the kids listen to me and do what I say?" Children are always watching what you're doing, and what you do sends a more powerful message to people than what you say. Ralph Waldo Emerson expressed it best when he wrote, "What you are stands over you the while, and thunders so that I cannot hear what you say to the contrary."

Much of wise leadership is about authenticity. In a visceral way, most people know an authentic leader from one who is inauthentic. They figure it out pretty quickly from the mixed signals they receive. It doesn't matter what kind of organization you're in; people pick up on that discrepancy right away, and they write off inauthentic people. So many leaders try to pump up what they're talking about without realizing that what they do belies what they say.

Actions Speak Louder Than Words

People see what you are by what you do, and they determine what you are by what they see—and they see actions. A level of comfort and acceptance are created when your actions and your words are in alignment. When there's a misalignment, a dissonance sets in that causes people to make a judgment about what to believe. What you do is *always* much more powerful than what you say. People can say anything, but the way they behave makes a much more powerful statement about what they are, what they stand for, what they believe, and what their values are.

The Harvard Urban Superintendents Program works with students on the issue of vision and mission, forcing them to think about clarifying their values so that they can exhibit those values in their own organizations. That kind of training is critical for leaders; if you're not aligning your behavior with the values you espouse, that lack of alignment quickly leads people to think, "I don't have to pay attention to that person because he doesn't mean what he says."

In her wonderful book, *My Grandfather's Blessings*, Rachel Remen raises the notion that we experience stress when our actions are out of alignment with our own spiritual nature. When our words and our deeds are not aligned, we may not only be diminishing our effectiveness as leaders, we may also be creating stress that is harmful to ourselves! It seems that not only do other people know when something is out of alignment between our words and our deeds, but our own *internal* system is aware of it. Moreover, when you are out of alignment, not only are you creating stress in your own life, but also in the lives of the people you're leading.

Wise Leaders Are Aware That Everyone Is Watching Them

Your behavior speaks volumes. When you're a leader, what you say is magnified far beyond what you may be able to see. People read your actions or lack of actions and draw their own conclusions. In many cases that's where Paul got into trouble—by *not* doing something, as opposed to doing what he did. People expect something; if you don't fulfill their expectations, they may react as if you meant something that you didn't mean. People are always watching you. You are always on stage, and the spotlight is on you simply because you're a leader. Sometimes that spotlight tends to shine more brightly than it should. So everything you do and say—every behavior and tic, every gesture and nuance—is magnified far beyond what you think possible. You are the bug under the microscope. Small actions are going to have big consequences because whatever you do is perceived to be bigger than it is. This is true for your affect as well as your actions.

Paul's face is genetically wired to look serious. His mouth turns down a bit and he has a frown line down the middle of his forehead, so in repose sometimes he can appear angry. Though he's not angry, people often perceive that he is, and then they respond according to that perception. They observe a frown line or a serious look and think, "He must be mad at me. What did I say? I must have done something wrong." They leap from an external perception to internalizing what they might have done to cause whatever it is that they believe. Wise leaders are aware not only that people are watching them, but also that the watchers frequently draw faulty inferences based on their own perceptions and internal assumptions.

Leaders Can Learn from the Observations of Children

Children are extremely authentic beings—almost to a fault. Sometimes, in fact, you may wish that they had a little less authenticity! Children can be brutally honest about the way they view the world. There's a tremendous alignment between what they see and say. What happens as we get older is that we learn to be much more *dis*honest and to cover our feelings and emotions and reactions with all sorts of layers, which only serves to confuse everyone around us. Often, however, we don't do a perfect job of covering up our true feelings or beliefs, and then people have to read the mixed signals that we send out. But children rarely send out mixed signals. Their signals are very clear.

Whether you're in the field of education or outside it, you're familiar with such phrases as "out of the mouths of babes" or "kids say the darnedest things." Many raw truths come out of children's mouths; at times we can actually benefit from seeing the world through their eyes. Often they see quite clearly and are not at all hesitant to say what they see. It's so interesting to observe how children deal with pretentious people or people who take themselves too seriously. Kids will explode such facades without even knowing that's what they've done, just because they don't have any room for such pretentiousness in their world. Children may give us a window on a truth we're not yet ready to hear but that nonetheless has validity. When you work with children, you come to realize that they are keen observers and that often what they say is quite accurate and worth considering. Wise leaders know that children have as much to teach us, their parents and leaders, as we have to teach them.

We Are Each Other's Role Models

We humans serve as each other's role models, whether or not we wish to do so. Earlier we raised the notion that people watch their leaders, but they also watch each other. At some level we are learning from each other all the time as we behave in different circumstances. The role-modeling issue becomes: Which of these behaviors do you make a conscious decision to emulate? We are all students of human behavior; we're always watching people and people are always watching us.

This modeling process occurs both consciously and unconsciously. It has been estimated that our unconscious mind has about nine times the processing capacity of our conscious mind for reading body language and other nonverbal cues. On either a conscious or an unconscious level, we are continually watching and assessing other people, comparing them to ourselves, and then trying to emulate or avoid selected qualities and behaviors we have observed. We are engaged in a continual process of teaching others by our example and learning from the examples of others, with or without conscious intent. Being aware of this process may help you move in the direction of wanting to model your best self for others. Everyone gets to lead at different times and in different ways, but one of the ways we lead is by being who we are and thereby influencing those around us by our very state of being.

There's a perception that leaders only lead if they have groups of followers. But sometimes leaders lead one at a time. *The wise leader knows that he or she can make a difference in the lives of people one at a time.* That opportunity is always available to you regardless of your role because, unless you're a hermit, you're always around other people, and like it or not, you have an impact on them.

Leaders Are Held to a Higher Norm

It has been our experience that leaders are held to a higher norm than the rest of society. Leaders need to be aware that they are role models all the time. They are held to the ideal of how we as a society or culture think people should be, and that becomes part of the leader's unwritten job description.

Behaviors that we would tolerate in other people we tend to tolerate less in leaders. The expectations for a leader's behavior tend to be higher; the forgiveness level, lower. (Yes, there *is* a double standard. It's not particularly fair, but it exists nonetheless.) If you're in a leadership position, you must take the bitter with the sweet. Certain things about being a leader are quite wonderful in terms of your sphere of influence; at times, you enjoy respect, prestige, and other perks and benefits.

But if you're going to enjoy all of the many benefits, then you must be willing to endure the other side of the coin, which is that you will probably be held to a different standard, and judged when you feel you shouldn't be judged, many times on inadequate information.

Unfortunately, when you're in a position of leadership, you're often judged without really being *known*. This happens because you're observed from afar, and people draw conclusions grounded in their own values. If they agree with something you've done, they like you; if they disagree, they tend to dislike you. If you did something they thought was hurtful to their particular cause, they tend not to like you. If you support their cause, they tend to like you. So in addition to being judged at a distance, you are held to a different standard in which "beauty is in the eye of the beholder." It's often unfair and sometimes painful, but it goes with the territory.

When We Walk Our Talk, People Listen

The continuum of walking our talk ranges from people who hardly ever walk their talk, to people who walk their talk sometimes, to people who walk their talk most of the time. On that continuum, the higher the degree of congruence between your walking and your talking, the more powerful you will be in terms of the way people listen to you. The people in the middle of the scale are moderately powerful; the ones at the far ends are either ignored altogether or very powerful.

Leaders whose walk and talk are absolutely congruent are quite rare. Steve is fortunate to have known two such people; both became his mentors—one when he was an undergraduate and the other when he was in his doctoral program. He was astounded by both people; he would listen to them and then observe and study them, both professionally and personally. Even as they became friends and he got to know them better and learn more about who they really were, he simply could not find any apparent inconsistencies between what they said and what they did. Not that they were perfect people—they made errors as we all do, but the degree of congruence between their walk and their talk was so high that it became a powerful motivator for him to want to learn from them and try to emulate them. Of all the people Steve has encountered, these two were the most comfortable in their own skins. Being comfortable in your own skin is being comfortable with who you are and behaving accordingly. That's something to strive toward; such people tend to be very balanced, productive, happy, and serve as useful role models for everyone around them.

Being Authentic

There's a relationship between a leader's level of wise leadership and his or her level of authenticity: the more authentic you are, the greater your potential to be a wise leader; the less authentic you are, the less likely it is that you will be a wise leader. In other words, you can't be a wise leader and be inauthentic. The whole notion of authenticity is linked to being who you really are; when you are who you really are, you tap into the divine aspect of yourself. That's also the source of your wisdom, so you're drawing from the same well. It's important for leaders to understand that powerful relationship.

How do you get to be authentic? It's a struggle. The journey toward authenticity is the same as the journey toward wise leadership. We have come to believe that you can start your journey in either place. You can work toward becoming a wise leader and find that you are becoming more authentic, or you can work at aligning your actions in the world with your true inner self and find that you are becoming a wiser leader.

While these two journeys are so entangled that each affects the other, authenticity may center on the issue of *psychological* health, while wise leadership focuses on the issue of *spiritual* health. The search for authenticity tends to be a psychological search; if you are successful, it allows you to go on to a spiritual search in a much more powerful and productive way.

One of our favorite writers is Wayne Dyer. Early in his career, Dyer focused primarily on psychological behavior; now, later in his career, he focuses on spiritual behavior. In many ways it's two ends of the same string. Which end of the string do you want to grasp first? The decision is yours, just as the journey is also uniquely yours.

The Importance of Honesty

We have found that, in those moments when we've been less than honest or when we have lost our sense of integrity, the world darkens. When we fall out of balance and become confused, the world becomes negative. On the other hand, when balance is regained and, along with it, that place of honesty and integrity, everything lightens up, everything falls into place—and we feel powerful!

As human beings, we are continually placed in positions that test our honesty and integrity. Paul recalls a time when he wasn't being true to himself as he struggled with the issues confronting him. He had allowed other people to make choices for him, as opposed to making his own choices. Even that was a choice he had made, and he didn't like the way it made him feel. He then made a different choice not to allow other people's judgments to control his behavior, and immediately he returned to a place where he felt a sense of integrity, authenticity, and honesty. As a result of his new resolve, he felt extremely powerful and light.

One aspect of authenticity has to do with who makes the choices. Who do you allow to make the choices in your life? Being comfortable in your own skin is making your own choices, as is not allowing other people's judgments to control your behavior, especially when those judgments are in conflict with your own values and principles. Making judgments for yourself, and guiding your own behavior based on your own values and principles, is the height of integrity.

The Importance of Your Word

Your word is the rock on which you stand. We are among those who believe that your word is your bond. But it's often helpful to put your words in writing, because memories can sometimes differ as to what the spoken words actually were, and because sometimes people hear what they want to hear, which may differ from what was intended. Sometimes we think we're being true to our word, but perhaps we really don't recall precisely what we actually said. Over the years, people have approached Steve and said, "By the way, you said such and such, but ..." And Steve has thought, "Hmmm, so I did." That becomes a time to make things right, or at least to explain why you didn't do what you said you would.

Very early in Paul's career, a friend of his became superintendent in a large city. Paul had just accepted a job as a building principal in another city. A week or so later, Paul's friend approached him about becoming the assistant superintendent in his new district. That was very heady stuff for a twenty-eight-year-old fresh out of graduate school. When Paul's friend said, "I need you," Paul replied, "I can't, because I've already told someone else I'm coming to work for him." In reality, Paul had not yet signed a contract, so he could have told his new employers that he had received a better offer, which was true since his friend had offered him a 50 percent salary increase—the difference between being an elementary principal in a small district and the assistant superintendent in a big district. But Paul had given his word. Instead, he said, "I can't go back on my word. I can't do that."

Sometimes walking your talk is hard, extremely hard, and sometimes it includes sacrifice, at least in the short term. Now, though, there is no question in Paul's mind that because he kept his word the universe rewarded him with a stellar career.

To become The Wise Leader:

- Know how important it is to walk your talk.
- Strive to bring your walk and talk into greater congruence.
- Be mindful that actions speak louder than words.
- Know people are always watching what you do and listening to what you say.
- See children as keen observers of the world around them.
- Know that we all serve as role models for each other.
- Understand that you are held to a higher norm.
- Be mindful that when you walk your talk people listen.
- Be authentic.
- Be honest.
- Be guided by your integrity.
- Keep your word.

CHAPTER 6

The Wisdom of Fighting for What's Right

Wise leadership is about knowing what's right and fighting for it. Wise leaders have an inner guidance system that helps them know what's right in a polarized and confusing world. Once they know what's right, wise leaders cannot turn away from what they know. They feel an obligation to do the right thing, and to fight for the right thing—even if, in the short term, their decision involves sacrifice and is detrimental to their own well-being. They understand that often the right path is the more difficult one, but that does not deter them.

When the Bush administration and Congress drafted the No Child Left Behind law, the American Association of School Administrators (AASA) discussed the proposed legislation with its members and concluded that the law had several serious flaws that would end up harming schools, harming children, and failing to accomplish its stated purpose. AASA sent a letter to the White House and to members of Congress outlining those aspects of the proposed law it saw as positive, as well as the elements that were ill-conceived and should be cut. Within a day AASA received a call from the White House saying, basically, "Who do you think you are to be sending this kind of letter?"

AASA's reply: "This is par for the course with major new educational legislation. We were trying to be helpful in giving the administration feedback about the proposed law."

The White House rejoinder, in effect, was: your job is to just get behind this law, support it, and not be critical.

"That's going to be difficult," replied the AASA representatives, "because our members think that certain portions need to be changed or eliminated."

When the proposed new law was not amended, AASA let it be known that it was not supporting it, despite concerns about possible repercussions. Almost immediately after passage of the law, AASA was shut out of discussions with the administration on virtually everything and had difficulty dealing with many people on Capitol Hill who had supported the law and therefore did not appreciate AASA's public stance.

On a personal level, Paul (who was then executive director of AASA) was ostracized in a variety of meetings and settings for fighting the law. Within the organization were a number of people who opposed AASA's position, but the vast majority of the membership supported it. Some people actually attacked Paul personally and tried to oust him from his job. One state commissioner of education visited the White House and, the following day, suggested to the superintendents in his state that they should cancel their membership in AASA. Because AASA had opposed this particular law as it was being drafted, there were personal vendettas as well as organizational vendettas. For example, when Paul was being considered for a prominent position at a major university, top-level officials in Washington intervened to make sure he did not get it.

As time has passed, AASA's position on the law now seems to be quite mainstream. Many people have come around to seeing the same flaws that AASA saw from the beginning. Today, questioning No Child Left Behind does not take a lot of courage; when it was first passed, however, the story was quite different. AASA and its executive director faced the decision of trying to fight for what they felt was right—to fight for what was in the best interest of its members and the children they serve. They paid a price for that battle; it would have been much easier not to take such a stand. But they believed, then as now, that to do otherwise would have been wrong. It was a good lesson for Paul and those who followed his lead—to know that there are times when you must stand up and be counted, and to know that even if your position is unpopular, or dangerous to you personally, you must still fight for what's right.

Why It Is Incumbent upon Leaders to Strive to Do What Is Right

It is incumbent upon any leader to do what's right. In anything you do, if you're acting in an enlightened manner you need to take the right path, but leaders should do what's right because they are responsible for other people. *Leadership is a pact between the leader and those who are being led.* In any situation in which you have a pact with other people, you should be striving to do what's right for those you serve.

Though everyone should strive to do what's right, the wiser the leader, the more he or she will have an awareness of what is right in any given situation. It is that awareness of what, in fact, is right that creates a special opportunity as well as a special obligation for leaders who are functioning in an enlightened way. They have an intuitive sense of knowing what's right, and frequently what they see as being right involves walking a difficult, sometimes perilous path.

As the saying goes, "Ignorance is bliss." But ignorance is also an opportunity to do less rather than more. If you are *not* ignorant, if you *do* know what's appropriate, then automatically you have an obligation that you did not have when you didn't know. Thus being a wise leader can be construed as being both a blessing and a burden. If it *is* a burden, however, it's a burden you are willing to shoulder because you derive a deep sense of satisfaction from doing what's right. You carry that mantle of knowing, and when you know, you cannot in clear conscience turn away from what you know.

"To whom much is given, much is required," the Bible tells us. Leaders are given a great deal in terms of perks and opportunities and recognition. They're also given a lot of responsibility, and a large part of that responsibility is doing the right thing despite looming difficulties and obstacles.

The Right Path Is Usually the More Difficult One

The right path is usually the more difficult one because it is the higher one. Because it is not traveled as frequently, there may be many more obstacles on it than on the lower, more well-trodden path. There's not as much air to breathe up there because it's a more rarefied place. Taking the high road often requires going against convention. It's always easier to go along with the crowd, but unfortunately the mode for the crowd tends to be the lowest common denominator. To go against that flow requires a great deal of strength and courage, and a willingness to stand up against great odds.

Paul has a little sign in his office that reads: "It's easy to drift when the current's swift, to lie in your boat and dream, but in nature's plan it takes a real man to paddle a boat upstream." Doing the right thing means paddling upstream. When Paul left the superintendency in Tucson, he told friends that in the whole time he was there he never made one decision where the pressure on him was to do the right thing. The pressure was always to do the wrong thing, and every act had to be made despite that pressure. It was indeed the more difficult road to take.

That brings to mind the title of M. Scott Peck's bestselling book, *The Road Less Traveled* (derived from Robert Frost's poem "The Road Not Taken"). If leaders are trying to make a decision between Path A and Path B, and if they really aren't sure which choice is the right one, more often than not the tougher path is the correct one. If you want a good indication of which path is the right one, pick the one that's overgrown. Wise leaders in all fields can know that they are taking the right road when their chosen road leads to the betterment of their organizations and, ultimately, to the betterment of the world.

Leaders Must Be Prepared to Pay a Price in the Pursuit of Righteous Ends

Leaders must always be prepared to pay a price in the pursuit of righteous ends. The price may involve job security, financial security, health, loss of family life, career advancement, a pay increase, or just a good night's sleep. The price varies, but it's always there. History is replete with wise, enlightened leaders who gave their lives for some higher purpose. Martin Luther King Jr., John F. Kennedy, Mohandas

Gandhi—all paid the ultimate price for taking the right road because the right road was so threatening to people.

The best way to mitigate this dynamic is to create balance in your own life. When you pay the price of pursuing righteous ends, your energy is on outflow, and ultimately that imbalance will wear you down. Therefore, while it's crucial to know that a price must be paid and that you will have to make some sacrifices, it's also important to understand that you need to find balance in your life so that the energy is not all flowing one way. Otherwise, you end up burning out, and burning up, very quickly.

Not only is it necessary to restore your energy, you must also conserve it if you are to fight the right battles. You cannot fight *every* battle. Many leaders don't fight for the right things. You need to be courageous about choosing the right battles to fight. There are times when, as a matter of principle or in regard to a truly critical issue, you may decide to put your job on the line. But that's something you don't want to do too often—perhaps only once or twice throughout an entire career. "Knowing when to hold them and when to fold them" is an important quality of an effective leader. Sometimes giving in makes sense, and at other times there's no price high enough for what it would cost you if you did give in.

Leaders Must Learn to Use Their Inner Guidance System to Navigate through Uncharted Territory

Everyone has an inner guidance system, but some people are more attuned to their inner voice than others. Your inner guidance system is what helps you decide which battles to fight, and whether the battle will be worth the costs. Accessing your inner guidance system also increases your chances of doing what's right, especially when you are in uncharted territory. But you have to listen to it, and carefully.

What are some ways of accessing your guidance system? One of Paul's methods involves an exercise in which he talks to his higher self. For him, it's like talking to a senior partner or a silent friend who carries part of the load. Things seem to be clearer or to align themselves better when he uses that method.

You may find yourself struggling with a tough decision, trying to figure out what's right or what's the wisest course of action in a given situation, but how often do you actually think of asking for guidance? Then the question inevitably becomes: "Who are you asking?" Well, who would *you* ask? Options abound. You can ask God, you can ask the universe, you can ask your higher self, you can ask an angel or a saint, you can ask an enlightened being, and on and on—either in the quiet of your own mind or aloud, depending on your comfort level and surroundings.

First, it helps to formulate your question or intention, and then you can consciously ask for assistance and guidance. The next step is to open yourself up and just put your question out there into the universe, and allow the universe to respond. The answer may come to you in a moment of insight, in your dreams, through your intuition, through your feelings, sometimes in your heart or gut, or the information may begin to flow from events or other people or through synchronicity. Regardless of the approach you choose, begin the process by asking.

Why It Is Incumbent upon Leaders to Protect Their Charges from Negative Energy and Undue Pressure

We live in a polarized universe where many people are not guided by what's good for others but instead are focused only on what's good for themselves. Such people frequently have power and put pressure on leaders to act in ways that are self-serving or to incur favor with a particular constituency, which may not serve the greater good or be beneficial in the long run (though it may look good in the short run). At times the pressure takes the form of negativity and its associated negative energies. Sometimes the effects of such pressure can negatively affect or be directed at people at every level of an organization. *One of our jobs as leaders is to protect the people we are leading.* It is incumbent upon us to absorb criticism and to run interference for others in our organization. To protect individuals or groups, wise leaders may at times choose to take a hit and figuratively jump in front of the negative energies that are being unleashed.

As a leader, you are like the center pole in a circus tent. Your job is to lift the canvas up off the backs of everyone under the tent. You are also creating a buffer to absorb the pressure that falls on people who are trying to get their work done, which allows them then to actually do their work rather than feel oppressed by all the demands coming down on top of them. A wise leader creates a buffer between negative forces and the people who are trying to do what's right, thereby providing protection. In a larger sense, the leader serves as a middleman, keeping things going in the right direction while simultaneously relieving the pressure from those in the trenches.

Leaders Must Stand Up to Small-Mindedness

Metaphorically, the devil doesn't arrive in a blaze of sound and fury; most times, in fact, he shows himself in small ways. Small-mindedness is a large part of what brings down the world. Day in and day out, it's the piling up of small things that creates the large things. By standing up to confront the small things, sometimes you can prevent the large things from taking place. *Stop negativity at its source.* Negativity is like the sand in the oyster—the oyster needs only a single grain of sand to become irritated. The small, petty acts that we face in our lives, the countless minor irritants, are really the things that create most of the problems. As a leader, you have to stand up against small-minded thinking and small-minded acts. The wise leader knows when and how to do so.

Since wise leaders tend to see further and from a larger perspective than many others, they're in a position to continually reframe the way issues are seen and to challenge small-mindedness. From a narrow field of vision, small-mindedness may appear to be correct, but the act of helping others to see things in a broader or more holistic context often reveals a larger truth.

One form of small-mindedness that's particularly corrosive is *narrow*-mindedness. Small minds and narrow minds can prove to be very destructive because they are not able to see the potential impact of events and actions on other people. When small- or narrow-minded people wield power, they have the potential to create a lot of damage, which is another reason why the threat they pose must be faced. Frequently such people display a deadly combination of ignorance and arrogance. They are willful, and they don't know that they don't know—which calls to mind the old joke in which one guy says to the other, "Why do you think there's so much ignorance and apathy in the world?" The other guy replies, "I don't know and I don't care."

Wise Leaders Do the Right Things as well as Do Things Right—All for the Right Reasons

An aphorism intended to explain the basic difference between managers and leaders observes that managers do things right while leaders do the right things. However, the "right things" for wise leaders go beyond the right things organizationally; they are the *morally* right things. Wise leadership is broader than just having proper personnel practices. It involves creating a culture that attracts people of the highest quality and then brings out the best in them in a way that serves both the individual and the organization.

Wise leadership is first doing no harm. It's seeing that people are allowed to grow. There are managers, leaders, and enlightened (i.e., wise) leaders. The right thing at the managerial level may include instituting effective systems and processes. At the leadership level, the right thing may include keeping the big picture in mind while taking care of the organization. At the enlightened level of wise leadership, the right thing becomes empowering the people in the organization to create the best possible future for the organization and its stakeholders.

Enlightened, wise leaders have to be able to manage at times, in the sense of doing things right, and to lead at times, in the sense of knowing the right things to do. They do so in a way that's attuned to serving the people they affect, but they must also be able to integrate those elements from a holistic perspective. An ordinary leader might do things in an organization that are managerially correct, so he would be doing things right. Or she could be doing things that are better for the organization, which would be doing the right thing. But there's still something missing. What's missing is the leader's *intention*, which underlies the action. At an even deeper level, what are the leader's core values and spiritual principles that drive his or her intention? In short, leadership needs to be performed for the right reasons, and these reasons must be rooted in core values and fundamental spiritual principles.

To become The Wise Leader:

- **Strive to do what is right.**
- **Know that the right path is usually the more difficult one.**
- **Be prepared to pay a price in the pursuit of righteous ends.**
- **Be courageous.**
- **Learn how to access and use your inner guidance system.**
- **Protect your charges from negative energy.**
- **Stand up to small-mindedness.**
- **Do the right things as well as doing things right, all for the right reasons.**

Part II

CHAPTER 7

The Wisdom of Knowing That Light Attracts the Dark

Bright Lights Make Good Targets

The essence of leadership is providing light to others. Wise leaders in particular must be a source of light to others. In a world of darkness, however, you do stand out. If someone has it in for you and bad intentions, you're an easy target. Leaders don't blend in very well. By definition, leaders *are* "outstanding." The more you stand out, the better target you become for those who may disagree with you or who do not like what you stand for. Sometimes the motive may be simple jealousy. Other times it is outright hostility to what you are trying to do. In either case your leadership makes you a target.

The brighter your light shines, the more likely it is that you'll be targeted by opponents. Wise leaders tend to upset the status quo. Those forces who wish to maintain the status quo or to move in a different direction are always poised to object and obstruct. They go after whomever and whatever threatens their position and philosophy. The first step is to weaken or get rid of the person leading the threat. In warfare, military people speak of "decapitating" the enemy. Most often they don't mean literal decapitation, but they do mean taking out the enemy's command-and-control structure. In day-to-day terms, decapitation is simply opposing and trying to take down the leader who threatens to make change.

Military strategy also calls for taking out the enemy's electrical grid. This disrupts communication and throws the opponent into darkness. Darkness creates confusion and misdirection and builds fear. Light gives people comfort and a sense of certainty. They can see what is happening, and they don't bump about aimlessly; they can go where they need to go. In organizations, if you don't like the direction the leader is going, you try to create a sense of darkness so that followers become confused and lost. That's why it is imperative for wise leaders to be certain that their light shines clearly in order to help their followers stay on course.

Darkness Is the Absence of Light and Is All About Ignorance

Think of light as a metaphor for the kind of leadership we are talking about—not necessarily a comforting, diffused light, but a spotlight that serves to direct people's attention to what is important. The light of leadership can also be thought of as that of torches and lanterns, which can be used to lead people to safety through the darkness. Or you might think of campfires, which welcome people in from the darkness and create a sense of community and security.

Light in today's culture brings to mind the myriad lightbulbs that light up our homes or offices. The lightbulb is also a symbol for ideas. When we get an idea, or an in*sight*, we envision a little cartoon lightbulb blinking on over our heads. So turning on a lightbulb is a metaphor for creating new ideas.

If light represents ideas, then the opposite represents the lack of ideas. When we say we're "in the dark" about something, we mean we are clueless and don't really know what's happening. Over and over, our language reminds us that light is about knowing and darkness is about not knowing. As we'll discuss in chapter 16, light is about hope and darkness is about fear.

The best example to illustrate the issue of darkness in society is the so-called Dark Ages. The Dark Ages weren't dark because the sun had dimmed. They were dark because people didn't know enough to improve their lives. They were a time of vast inequality between serfs and lords, a time when raw power ruled and learning was not available to most people. They were a time when the majority of people were ignorant. After the Dark Ages came the Age of Enlightenment, when the arts flourished and learning was revered. People came into the light. Our history is filled with darkness and light.

It is important to remember, though, that darkness is the absence of light. Darkness does not even exist as a concept without being defined by light. As long as there is light there cannot be darkness. But darkness is always working against light and trying to draw it in—like a black hole. In our relationships and organizations we meet people who act as black holes, who suck the light from us. Darkness is not without power—it has the power to draw energy from light, and leaders must always be vigilant to prevent that from occurring.

Wise Leaders Will Continually Encounter Negative Energy

We know that life is made up of polarities: good and bad, right and wrong, male and female. Light and darkness are another set of polarities; they constitute the yin and yang of positive and negative forces. Wise leaders who show vision and positive energy will almost inevitably attract negative energy, which will be arrayed against them. Wise leaders don't plan it that way. That's just the way it is. In hunting, the buck with the greatest antlers becomes the prized target. In organizations, the leaders with the biggest ideas are targeted.

We have always wondered where so many negative people come from! We certainly have not aimed to create them, but we do seem to draw them to us. In fact, it's rather astounding how many people don't see themselves as having a stake in making things better. They seem content to let the status quo remain as it is—or even to act in ways that make matters worse. These are people who seem to see their success in terms of stopping others.

Wise leaders are energized by doing things that help other people; they try to generate positive energy in other people. Unenlightened leaders, on the other hand, seem to be energized by diminishing others and by generating negative energy. They are self-absorbed, self-centered, and selfish. They seem motivated to take energy that could go toward the common good and appropriate it for their own purposes. The difference between a wise leader and one who is not is the difference between a leader whose energy is flowing outward and one whose energy is pulling inward. Black holes pull light in; stars give off light. One is constricting and pulls everything toward itself; the other beams light outward. One acts selfishly; the other, selflessly.

Wise leaders need to understand that the universe seems to be constructed in such a way that these countervailing forces of light and darkness are entangled. Positive, creative energy attracts negative energy like a light draws bugs. In both physical and spiritual ways, opposites *do* attract. Understanding this duality can free the wise leaders from thinking that when they encounter opposition it is because they did something wrong. In fact, it is often true that the more opposition a leader experiences, the more likely it is that he or she did something very right.

It is also important to understand that this phenomenon is natural. It's not about you, so don't make the mistake of personalizing it. When you encounter opposition, it's good to remember that it probably isn't about you—the *personal* you. It's about the grander you, the one who is trying to lead toward the light. When you find yourself faced with an array of negative forces, you should feel comforted; that's a pretty good sign that you are trying to do the right thing. Some believe that you should be proud of the friends you make, but even prouder of the enemies you make. Here's a simple guideline for any leader to use: if you're alienating people you admire and like, and attracting people you would normally oppose, you are probably on the wrong track. But if you're alienating people who are selfish, negative, and just plain obstinate, then full speed ahead!

Once, when Paul had made a joke in public that some saw as racially tinged (even though it certainly was not), he was attacked pretty severely. Sadly, his attackers were people he could normally count among his supporters, people who he wished to help. Even worse, he was being cheered on by some notable racists in the community! That's when Paul knew that he needed to apologize publicly for what he had said, even though he had been misunderstood. He didn't want the backing of those who were supporting him on this issue; he knew that his values and theirs were not aligned and that those who were attacking him on this issue actually shared his beliefs. So he apologized publicly and, further, announced that he was stepping down from his position. When the leader of the group who had been attacking him came to him with tears in her eyes and begged him to stay, he knew he had taken the right course.

When you take a principled position, some will always oppose you. When you try to please everyone, you stand for nothing. Sometimes wise leadership is not rewarded in the moment, but it is still always the right path to take.

When you are confronted with opposition that helps define you and what you stand for, the conflict also helps to define your opposition. The stakes become very clear. It is good for a wise leader to try to stay in the moment. In fact, we devote a whole chapter to that issue later in this book (see chapter 13). When you can take a more systemic and less personal approach, you can stay in the moment and be both a participant in the action and, simultaneously, an observer of it. This creates a detachment that allows your vision to remain much clearer and more pure. You are less emotionally engaged in the roller-coaster of events and can see things from a broader perspective. That stance allows you to act more wisely. Detachment allows you to avoid being pulled into the dark energy opposing you. If you allow yourself to remain attached to the forces that confront you, you are subject to them. Pull back to a position of detachment, however, and you are still aware of what is happening, but not simply reacting to it. You become an actor, not a reactor.

Leading with Light Requires Openness

Consider the metaphor of a lens. It is necessary for the lens to be open to let in light. Similarly, to *lead* with light, a leader must be open. Fear stems from darkness. When we are small we are afraid of the dark. Darkness covers the unknown. When you are in a dark place, fear surrounds you. When you are able to turn on the light, the monster in the closet may be only an overcoat. When you bring light to bear you realize that much of what held you back or created hesitancy simply isn't worth that effort. Openness is impossible when you are fearful. Openness acts as a countermeasure to fear. Wise leaders must embrace the world, and that simply cannot be done when fear is present. Openness drives out fear. Openness is active; fear is passive.

We see this duality played out constantly in the sphere of politics. We see people who are fearful of immigrants, or of those who have an alternative lifestyle. Someone who is different threatens such people and makes them fearful. Openness to differences allows us to see the beauty in everyone—even those who may be different. Leading with light requires us to be open to the possibilities that life presents. We find beauty in the diversity that surrounds us and power in the unexpected gifts that come when we are open.

The Interplay between Darkness and Light Can Create Focus and Intensity

Keep in mind the ways in which a painter uses light. You'll notice that an artist who uses light masterfully—Rembrandt, for instance—is also a master at using darkness. The darker areas of the painting give the lighter areas definition and power. The interplay of light and shadow makes a more powerful image. Light needs the contrast with darkness to show itself fully.

As leaders, we should always be grateful for the dark times we face; they give added meaning to the lighter ones. It helps us to be less afraid of the dark when we realize that darkness helps define our light. The interplay of forces and contrasts puts things in perspective;

the contrast becomes apparent between those things that enhance and empower and those that diminish and disempower.

We have suggested that wise leaders must learn how to focus light. Sometimes they must focus the light on the darkness to show it for what it is. While darkness reveals light, light also reveals darkness and what lies within it. By revealing what is in the darkness, we find that either our fears or concerns were unfounded or that sometimes something lurks there that must be confronted and addressed. Leaders help their followers to distinguish between shadow and substance. Sometimes shadows are just shadows, but sometimes they can mask a formidable challenge. Wise leaders know the difference and help others see that difference.

Leaders Can Take Advantage of Trials and Tribulations

It is wise to remember that trials and tribulations are really just lessons and opportunities dressed up in wolves' clothing. If we accept the premise that life demands that we be lifelong learners, then we must also accept the fact that many of life's greatest lessons come from the troubles we face. Certainly there are positive lessons (many of them fairly easy) that allow us to learn. But many of our lessons are hard and not always pleasant.

Leaders know that they will face trials. Over time, these trials will take different forms. But every lesson creates an opportunity. Trials and tribulations should cause us to reflect before we react. Often the process of reflection reveals the lesson to be learned. Less wise leaders attempt to avoid trials and tribulations. They seek a smoother path and resist the lessons. Wise leaders learn to embrace the opportunity presented by the trial, whatever its nature, because they know they will grow as a result of it. When you resist lessons, the trials you face will grow bigger and the hills, steeper to climb. The energy you put into resistance enables the problem to grow. This exchange of energy can also work in positive ways. When you embrace a problem, you draw energy from it and grow stronger.

Leaders Must Have an Awareness of Evil and Be Prepared to Confront It

Wise leaders must remember that what they don't know can rise up and bite them. For some, the notion of evil is difficult to accept because it has heavy religious connotations. However, it's not hard to see that there are actions in the world that are so despicable and damaging and that exist for no good reason, that they can only be considered evil—even without the necessity of accepting the notion of heaven and hell or God and the Devil. Hitler was evil. Charles Manson was evil. Their actions affected the world in profoundly negative ways. Some have suggested that evil is the taking of life or liveliness from others; whether it be on a macro or a micro level, there are people who derive their own joy by taking it from others. If you are uncomfortable with the word "evil," call it something else. What we are talking about here is the fact there are forces and people in the world that exist for no good reason or that are acting in ways that are not beneficial to others; if you are a leader you are going to run into them.

M. Scott Peck, in his wonderful book *People of the Lie*, suggests that evil exists at the intersection of extreme narcissism and extreme willfulness. He suggests that evil grows from those who are so focused on themselves that they have no empathy for others and yet are committed to affecting others' lives in order to get their own way. Think about this: "evil" spelled backward is "live." Viewed from this perspective, evil is the opposite of all that we would want to see in our lives and the lives of those whom we love or are responsible for. Evil is the opposition to life. It is the responsibility of wise leaders to bring life to others. For that reason, they must confront and confound evil.

Leaders will constantly be confronted by forces that would take life away from those around them. Most spiritual traditions believe that goodness involves helping others. The opposite of goodness does the opposite. You know it when you see it. Because wise leaders attract this kind of energy, they constantly face the challenge of how to handle this "dark force." Leaders must learn how to block the impact of these people on their psyches and find ways to replenish their own positive energy. Wise leaders must learn how to protect themselves.

Paul and Steve both served for many years as public school superintendents. In that capacity they attended thousands of school board meetings. Often these meetings ended up becoming contentious and controversial, either because of individual board members who represented narrow and selfish agendas or because some member of the public came bearing a specific grudge. It was impossible to avoid the negative energy in such settings. However, both Paul and Steve found that a visit to a kindergarten classroom the following morning did wonders for their psyches and replenished their positive energy. There's nothing better than a room full of five-year-olds to remind you of life's possibilities.

Dealing with Negative Energy

Wise leaders must stay strong and resilient. They have to be prepared physically, mentally, emotionally, and spiritually to confront the constant flow of negative energy that will come their way. If there is weakness in some area of their lives—whether caused by a family issue or illness—they are more vulnerable to being overcome by negative forces.

When you encounter situations that should be clear and you find them becoming increasingly murky, then you may well be confronting dark forces, which use deception and confusion as tools. Wise leaders aim to create clarity out of confusion. Negative energies left unchecked will invariably grow and expand. Wise leaders understand the necessity of constantly confronting these energies.

Finally, remember that whether you characterize what we are talking about here as good versus evil, or the interplay between negative and positive energy, or the forces of light and darkness, they will be around you if you choose to lead. Deepak Chopra once described leadership as learning to step out of the darkness. Wise leaders understand that they will, by virtue of their actions, become targets for opposition. They will be surrounded by darkness and they must learn to step out of it and let their light shine. They must learn how to stay the course and do their duty. They can improve their chances of doing this if they understand the interplay of darkness and light.

To become The Wise Leader:

- Be mindful that bright lights make good targets.
- Know that darkness is the absence of light.
- Be aware that darkness is associated with ignorance.
- Expect to encounter obstacles and countervailing negative energy.
- Know that leading with light requires openness.
- See the interplay between darkness and light as a way to create focus, sharpness, and intensity.
- See trials and tribulations as lessons and opportunities.
- See evil as real and be prepared to confront it.
- Seek to counteract negative or dark energy.
- Generate positive energy in others.
- Be energized by helping others.
- Protect others from dark energy.

CHAPTER 8

The Wisdom of Balance

Leadership is a balancing act. The image of the acrobatic circus clown comes to mind. You know, the one with a half-dozen or so plates spinning precariously atop wooden dowels. The performer must start each plate spinning and then give each one enough attention to keep it going while adding new plates to the mix. Fail to maintain the proper balance and we all know what happens. *Crash, bang!*

Wise leaders are attuned to balance and understand its far-reaching importance within themselves, their organizations, and the way they lead. As impressed as we might be with the acrobatic clown, the balancing act for leaders is far more challenging. Leaders must maintain their own physical, mental, and emotional balance while being attuned to those same issues within the entire organization. What happens to people and organizations when leaders are emotionally or mentally unbalanced? What happens when leaders cannot find the right balance between the demands of their careers and their personal lives? What happens when leaders do not have the health, stamina, and energy needed to function effectively? Time management, stress management, resource management—all are related to the issue of balance. Leadership styles themselves can be too tight, too loose, or just right.

When you are a leader, you can be out of many things, but one of the things you don't want to be out of is balance. Invariably, when you or some aspect of your organization is out of balance, something undesirable happens. Wise leaders work at maintaining balance throughout their organization, but when something is amiss they take a closer look to see if an underlying imbalance is at the root of it.

Steve recalls a time when a decision not to grant tenure to a teacher caused an unexpected upheaval in his school district. On the surface, the issue seemed pretty clear-cut. Evaluation records showed that the teacher failed to meet district standards. However, the faculty reaction was so intense (and out of balance) that Steve met with faculty representatives to get a better sense of the underlying dynamics. It turned out that the faculty felt that the evaluation system itself was unfair (in other words, out of balance). Rather than viewing this issue as a power struggle, Steve reversed himself about the teacher in question and put a process in place to revise the entire evaluation system. Appropriate action calmed the turbulence and restored balance and equanimity.

Being Centered

Being centered is being in balance. When you're centered there's a sense of having both feet on the ground and having yourself in alignment and in balance, psychologically and energetically. Balance represents stability. Think of the center of gravity of an object; it's the point at which forces are the most balanced. The most-balanced leaders are those who offer stability to their organizations and to those around them. As leaders, we are pulled in many directions;

there is a frenetic aspect to our lives. Nonetheless, in the midst of all the forces swirling around us we must work at staying centered. We have to be able to project calmness and focus regardless of what may be occurring at any given moment. The leader's focused presence sets the tone for the organization and instills confidence. Steve remembers (from an internship in Newark, Delaware) overhearing heated discussions among the superintendent, the board president, and members of the staff. When the next person arrived for a meeting, however, there was no trace of the turmoil that had occurred only moments before. The superintendent could re-center himself at will.

Breathing exercises, yoga, and meditation are techniques we can use to center ourselves both mentally and energetically. But being centered is more than a frame of mind; it is a philosophy that goes back thousands of years to the ancient Greeks. They called it the Golden Mean—not going too far in any one direction. You didn't go to extremes in anything; you held to the Golden Mean: a centered place that gave you a sense of balance in all things. This recurring theme can be found in many traditions, including Buddhism, where it is called the Middle Path. The Middle Path holds that almost anything, taken to an extreme, can become bad or perverse, even things that we think of as good or desirable. We believe that wise leaders are well served by these ancient principles.

Energy Flows Freely When Systems Are Balanced

Wise leaders strive to create balance in all aspects of their organizations. They look at their organizations as systems and understand that in systems things flow more freely when the various elements are in balance. We also believe this precept. We have found that we need to be in balance for our own energy to flow freely. One way to create balance in our own selves stems from having a holistic view that encompasses mind, body, and spirit. If we want our energy to flow freely, we actually have to provide the opportunity for renewal and restoration in all three of these elements because there is a natural tendency for them to become unbalanced.

In fact, life itself seems designed to push us in the direction of imbalance. Scientists call this phenomenon the *law of entropy*. Entropy is the force that causes all things in the universe, including us, to break down and move toward a state of disorder. We may be fairly well balanced in our thinking but gradually, over time, we will find ourselves out of balance. We may be in balance physically, but again, over time, unless we are vigilant, our bodies will become less balanced. The same tendency holds true for our spirit.

Therefore, it's necessary to maintain balance *within* each of these three elements, but it's also necessary to keep a balance *among* these elements. Doesn't this call to mind the circus clown juggling the whirling plates? Constant adjustments among the three elements, and *balance*, are called for. True balance requires strategies, activities, and exercises to produce that effect in all three areas.

With respect to energy, leaders are on outflow most of the time. People come to leaders for support and for guidance. They come to you for ideas. They come to you for moral courage. They come to you for resources. Sometimes they come to you for energy. People would often walk into Paul's office when they were down or demoralized and say, "I just need to talk." Only rarely do visitors bring you things that will energize you. The leader's energy tends to flow out, not in. The metaphor we find most fitting is that people are dipping their bucket into your well. If you're not vigilant, you can wake up one morning and realize that your well has been drained dry. Everybody dipped their bucket into your well and you haven't taken the time to refill it. Wise leaders create practices for themselves that refill their well.

Balanced Systems Maximize Energy Output

As leaders we have an interest in fostering efficiency. We're interested in efficiency for ourselves because we want to use our energy wisely, so that it produces the greatest effect. We're very interested in making our organizations as efficient as possible, not only because the people whom we serve expect and demand it, but also because the reality of scarce resources creates an imperative for leaders to operate efficiently in order to leverage resources. We know the importance of this need, but how do we achieve it?

One secret is creating balanced systems. We must view our mind-body-spirit as a single integrated system, and our organization as a system, and the organization's place in the larger societal environment as part of an interconnected system. We need to realize that we can control only certain spheres of influence, but in the spheres that we do control we need to use lenses that help us see if the system is balanced. Is something out of kilter that's causing us or our organization to operate inefficiently? Are some aspects of the system strong and thriving while others are weak and starving? We can look at each aspect of ourselves and our organization and ask, *Do we have balance?*

Wise leaders engage in systems thinking and think about the interrelatedness of things. As a systems thinker you need to look at each subsystem to see that it is balanced. Furthermore, you need to see that the subsystems are in balance with each other. As the leader you can also help the people in your organization to think in these same terms and help them come to realize that everyone gains by being a part of a system that's operating coherently in a balanced fashion.

We want to be clear that we are not talking about achieving some sort of equilibrium for the purpose of standing still. What we're suggesting is balancing things for the purpose of moving forward. Think of an airplane that has been designed so that all of its systems and subsystems are in balance. When energy is applied to propel the plane it can fly straight and efficiently. If the plane is not balanced— possibly it has lost an engine—then it will not fly straight without compensating for the loss and it certainly won't fly efficiently. Or picture a person walking across a tightrope. They're balanced and yet they're moving forward. That's the image. It may feel precarious to imagine being on a tightrope, yet if you're balanced you can move forward even in dangerous circumstances. We suggest that balance creates the opportunity for maximum and efficient energy output, but *then* you need an intention or plan to take advantage of the balanced condition. Forward movement comes from a base of being balanced and centered.

Ways Leaders Can Foster Balance in Their Lives

If you live your life out of balance there's usually a price to be paid—often a severe price. Sometimes the price is simply a diminution in the quality of your life, or a shorter life span. Being aware that you are out of balance is the starting point. Then you must develop the tools needed to get into balance—whether that's an active reading life, exercising, creating nutritional balance, taking vacations, or using down time to do something other than working. At times it may even be beneficial for leaders to take a twenty-minute power nap.

In addition to the power nap, a leader can profit from taking a brief ten- or fifteen-minute walk in the middle of the workday to get his body moving and get some fresh air. Or he can simply close the door to his office and hold his calls so he can meditate, or do some deep belly breathing or stretching for five or ten minutes. Even the act of sitting quietly for a few minutes and focusing on one's breath can have healthy effects.

Closing off the normal frenetic environment and mental processing for ten minutes doesn't sound like much, but it can have significant payoff in terms of renewed energy, focus, and sense of well-being. It's easy to say, "I'm so busy, and under so much pressure, that I don't have ten minutes for such activities," but we predict you'll find that you have gained time rather than squandered it in terms of productivity, efficiency, and effectiveness. Wise leaders tell themselves, and those for whom they're responsible, that taking ten minutes for balancing and centering in the middle of the workday is not only okay, but it can actually help you to be more effective and productive.

One of Steve's professors once taught him that we all have the same amount of time to work with: twenty-four hours each day. He taught Steve that the real issue isn't so much our time as our priorities. In his book *Seeds of Greatness,* Dennis Waitley suggests that we look at different aspects of our lives as part of a wheel of balance; each pie-shaped slice of the wheel represents a different aspect of our lives. One slice may represent our work lives, another our personal lives, another our health, another our financial health, and still others our spiritual health, family life, recreation, and so forth. We can look at

Waitley's wheel (or one that we create for ourselves) and begin to see the areas that are not getting enough of our time. At that point it comes down to our values and priorities in terms of our willingness to shift time from one slice of the pie to another.

Our Vulnerability to Negative Energy Increases When We Are Out of Balance

The notion that our vulnerability to negative energy increases when we are out of balance really struck home with Paul. Spontaneously, he shared the following insight with Steve: "I'll tell you something funny," he admitted. "When I get out of balance, I get out of balance. I mean I literally get *out of balance.* About twice a year I have these episodes of vertigo. I realize now that when I get them, I need to reexamine everything because I am literally out of balance. It's usually because things have speeded up in my life, and I'm not attending to stuff, and I will get physically out of balance. It's the funniest thing, but now I know that when I get physically out of balance I've got to stop and take stock because it's really the rest of my life that's out of balance, not just my body. And as soon as I can get everything pulled back into shape the vertigo goes away. You talk about your body sending you a message. How much more literal can it be?"

When we become ill, usually our body is telling us something. For the most part, when we get ill it's because there's some aspect of us that's not sufficiently in balance or strong enough to withstand the negative energy or toxicity that may reside within us or around us.

When you are out of balance you are vulnerable. Imbalance creates the conditions for bad things to enter your life—things that you don't want to have in there: negative energy and illness. When you are vulnerable, that vulnerability is capitalized on by the very thing that you don't want to have in your life.

Reflecting on this dynamic, Paul said that when he is having a bad run of things in areas of his life, he tries to stop and figure out how to pull himself back into balance, and then those negative things will ease off and go away. When he is beset by numerous bad and negative forces he has to regroup and go back to basics—start exercising a bit more, getting a bit more sleep, doing more spiritual reading, getting involved in some intellectual exercise that takes him out of what he's been dealing with, eating healthier food. And when he starts doing these things suddenly the vulnerability and the danger he had been feeling starts to diminish and disappear.

Paul's insight is a very effective way of fighting negative energy and negative circumstances. Wise leaders know that one antidote they can employ to counteract negative forces and events is to engage in practices that will bring them back to a more balanced state of being.

Lessons from the Metaphor of a Seesaw

Picture a seesaw or teeter-totter. All of us can picture what it looks like when it's balanced—its beam is parallel to the ground. The seesaw will remain in a stable position so long as the forces on each side continue to be balanced. We also understand how easy it is for that seesaw to get out of balance; it doesn't take much to shift its balance one way or the other. This simple toy can help us appreciate how hard it is to remain in balance; one side or the other usually begins to exert a greater force and we see the seesaw shift—one side rising and the opposite side falling. It's easy to see that you can simply add more weight to the side that is up until it comes back into balance again. Weight is a metaphor for additional resources or energy; add additional resources or energy to the side that is up and balance is created once again. Another possibility, if you (or your organization) is out of balance, is to subtract resources or energy from the side that is down, thus restoring balance. Leaders are constantly considering what must be added or subtracted to help create the desired state of balance.

When the seesaw is close to being in balance the action is easy. When it's out of balance, a lot of work is required. Two children of the same weight can go up and down very easily with minimal effort, but as you move toward a lack of balance, much more effort is needed to keep moving. We think that organizations work in much the same way. When you have balance in your organization, and balance in your leadership style, it's easy to move things. The more out of balance the various factors become, the more difficult it is to keep the organization in balance and moving forward.

Another way of creating balance is to shift the fulcrum. Less weight (or force) is needed to balance a greater weight or force if you're on the longer side of the fulcrum. Therefore, one way of counteracting a greater force is to increase the length of the beam on your side of the fulcrum. Does this recall the high school physics lesson about Archimedes? He said, "Give me a lever long enough and a fulcrum on which to place it and I'll move the world." In our own way, as leaders, we're always trying to move the world, or at least the part of it for which we're responsible. The metaphor of the long lever helps us see that in any given situation leaders can focus on moving the fulcrum to leverage their energy to balance or move a greater force.

How the Principle of Balance Applies to Our State of Being and Our Capacity for Doing

Being and doing are intertwined. It's not just being a leader and acting as a leader that's important; it's about being the *kind* of leader that you need and want to be: a wise leader. When you achieve a sense of balance between what you do and who you really are, then you're going to move things in a good direction. You're going to be able to function more effectively. If you get out of balance, and you think it's all about you or what you do and you don't understand the importance of a sense of service to the organization or to the people around you as well as to yourself—then it's easy to go astray.

Sometimes we may be more focused on our being and other times we may be more focused on our doing. When the two elements are in harmony and integrated we function most effectively, but the principles of balance (and don't forget entropy) can affect them over time. As a result, sometimes you could be more of a doer and not so much in touch with your inner self, or you may be in touch with your inner self but may not be using what you know to the full extent that you could. So we have to be mindful that both elements are important and that over time we can come to achieve a better balance between them.

When we talk about wise leaders, we mean those leaders who are very much in touch with the *inner being* part of themselves. A great many people are focused primarily on doing. We agree with the saying that "managers *do things right*, while leaders also know *the right things to do*." In our view, however, wise leaders know the right things to do *and* do things right—but they do both for *the right reasons*. And those right reasons come from the *being* part of us. You are here on this world not to be a superintendent or a CEO or an executive director. That may be what you *do*. But what you are here to *be* is a contributor to the human race and to make our planet a better place because you have been here.

When you consider the kinds of issues we have been discussing in this chapter, you can learn how to tune into the being part of who you are, which is unique for each of us. It's your own being, your essence, that we firmly believe is connected to the divine. It's your own being that's connected to divine wisdom, and it's your own being that can guide and inform you as to your life's purpose and unique gifts.

Life Shows Us When We Are Out of Balance

As we mentioned earlier, Paul knows he is out of balance when he experiences dizziness. Life has a way of slapping us around when we are out of balance. If life is slapping you around, it's probably because you aren't paying attention to something to which you need to be paying more attention. The more you resist the signals life is sending you, the louder those warning signals will become.

In other words, life will just keep smacking you until you listen. These signals may be health related, work related, relationship related, family related, or from the exigencies of life. In a way, it's a very practical system for getting your attention because there are alarms that go off. It's like the smoke detector in your house. If you're burning the beans, the alarm will go off. We have a great many smoke detectors in our lives that remind us that we have to start paying attention. The important thing is not to focus on the smoke detector but to focus on the burning beans. In many cases, when the alarms go off we tend to focus on the alarm rather than on what's causing the smoke.

If you're exhausted most of the time, if you're sick very often, if your family relationships are deteriorating, if things at work are mostly not going well—all of these may be signals that you are out of balance in some area of your life. You need to be alert to pick up the signals that are coming in. If you can read life's signals and understand them early enough, sometimes only a minor shift is needed to create a better balance. If you ignore the signals, something that is minor and manageable can escalate into something that is less manageable and far more difficult to balance.

Wise leaders know that when life is not going well it's time to step back, look at the big picture, try to figure out what is out of balance, and then address it.

To become The Wise Leader:

- Work at being centered and being in balance.
- Know that energy flows more freely when systems are balanced.
- Know that balanced systems maximize energy output.
- Be mindful that exercise, good nutrition, rest, vacations, belly breathing, meditation, fun, and relaxation help create balance.
- Be mindful that dark forces and negative energy can knock you over when you are out of balance.
- Know that on a seesaw or in life you can add force, subtract force, or move the fulcrum to create balance.
- Be aware of the being part of yourself.
- Know that the principle of balance applies to your state of being as well as to what you do.
- Know that life shows you when you are out of balance.

CHAPTER 9

The Wisdom of Empowering and Uplifting Others

True leadership involves an exchange between leaders and followers. Wise leaders empower other people and are thereby empowered by them. The role of a leader is to help others understand their own power and unleash it.

Wise leaders have the ability to cultivate the power of those around them. They understand that when they give power away to others it comes back to them and enhances their own leadership abilities. They achieve this alchemy by recognizing power in others—sometimes power that those within the organization do not know they possess—and then creating an environment that allows them to manifest this power. Leaders who have trouble delegating responsibility and want to micromanage their organization do so because they do not trust the innate power of others, and they are unwilling to forgive them for not doing things in the same way the leader would. Wise leaders are willing to take risks to empower others. Success comes over time, and it comes from the growth of the people in the organization.

Every encounter we have with others is an opportunity to empower another person. Such empowerment requires trust and support. In fact, empowering others is so energizing and contagious that under the right circumstances it will spread like a virus throughout an organization. The essence of empowerment is helping others evolve continually into better and better versions of themselves. Wise leaders bring out the best in others by giving them permission and confidence to be themselves. The essence of empowerment is the desire to make others independent rather than dependent. A leader who wants to be surrounded by sycophants may feel better about his or her own power but is actually undermining the potential of the organization. This type of leader is not allowing his or her colleagues to become independently powerful people. Moving away from a command-and-control model that focuses on the leader to a service-and-support orientation focusing on others' leadership leverages the available human capital and human potential. The result is a stronger organization.

At the end of Paul's first year as a superintendent, a veteran principal came to see him. The principal told Paul that he was exhausted; he said he had never worked so hard in his career as he had that year because he had felt such great pressure to improve and succeed. The principal went on to say that he couldn't think of a time when Paul had actually ordered him or pushed him to work harder. Then the principal added that, as he had thought about it, he realized that the pressure he felt had come from Paul's expressing how much he valued the principal and how much confidence he had in him. That had caused the principal to pressure *himself* to do his best because he knew that it was in him to do it, and if he slacked off, he was cheating himself.

Paul heard this message repeatedly from those he led during his career. Why? Because Paul really did believe in others and their ability to rise to the occasion. It wasn't an artifice or a gimmick—he genuinely believed in the possibilities of those around him. As Paul faced his own retirement he realized that whatever legacy he left behind was not in the programs he started or the buildings he built— it was in the hearts and minds of people. Real leaders, if they are empowering leaders, leave a little of themselves in everyone around them. Micromanagers are quickly forgotten.

How Can Wise Leaders Use Their Own Gifts to Empower Others?

Part of the path to empowering others is for the leader to be open and generous of spirit. That openness allows others the freedom to take hold of what they need to do to better themselves. A wise leader knows his or her people and helps them find what they need. Phil Jackson, the storied coach of the Chicago Bulls and the Los Angeles Lakers, at the beginning of each season gave every one of his players a book. Each book was different, and every player came to understand that what was in his own particular book was a message from Phil about something that could make him a better player. Jackson's leadership was rewarded with more NBA championships than any other coach in the history of the game. Wise leaders know what others need and make it possible for them to possess it.

Moreover, wise leaders free people to use their own gifts. Again Coach Jackson provides an example of wise leadership: during a game he was eerily calm on the bench; he seemed able to manage the very different and very large egos among his players and get the best out of each one because he created an atmosphere of expectation— that each player would use his talents to the best of his ability and that the combination of the whole team's talents would be enough to win. Jackson did not handle Dennis Rodman, for instance, in the same way that he handled Michael Jordan.

It is critical for the leader to say, "It's all right for you to be you." That statement is an incredibly empowering message! Scientists believe that most of us use only a fraction of our potential. When a leader says, "You have great things to offer," and then creates a climate in which those great things can happen, *great things result.* Wise leaders give others permission to try. Wise leaders give people permission to be themselves. Leaders do not give power to people; they allow the power that is already there to blossom. The lyric in the oldie by the rock group America—"Oz didn't give nothing to the Tin Man that he didn't already have"—shows the Wizard of Oz to be a wise leader. The Scarecrow already had a brain; he just didn't realize it until he was told he had it. The Cowardly Lion was far from cowardly, and the Tin Woodman had a heart long before he met the Wizard. The Wizard, despite his shortcomings, was a wise leader because *the wise leader gives others the gift of themselves.* Wise leaders are not paragons of perfection. They are simply smart enough to see qualities in others that they may not see themselves and then create conditions in which those qualities can be put to good use.

Empowering others really is easy. Allowing people to be themselves doesn't take a lot of effort—it just takes the ability to let go and trust.

Uplifting Others

The best way to uplift others is to lift the weight from them. The result is much like a hot-air balloon jettisoning its sandbags. Without the extra weight, the balloon soars. Wise leaders understand the sandbags in their organization and try to get rid of them. Every "you can't" or "you shouldn't" or "it's against the rules" keeps the organization from soaring.

Steve fondly remembers one of his mentors, Lee Olsen, who reminded Steve frequently that whenever you interact with another human being, you have, if only for a moment, the opportunity to enhance or diminish that person's self-concept. That moment does not depend on your role in the organization. It is present in every interaction we have with others. What power we possess! We can raise others up or tear them down.

Wise leaders learn how to build rather than demolish. Being aware that this process of building up and empowering others is constantly occurring, and being aware of how our words and deeds affect others—these factors help us understand that when we interact with others we do so at two levels. First, there is the content of the interchange—that is, the practical aspect of the interaction. But second, and equally important, there is also a subtext or the *way* we interact that tells other people if we appreciate and value them, or if we see them as only another resource to be used. Every interaction is an opportunity to enhance or diminish.

Some remarkable people seem able to uplift others consistently. Nelson Mandela and the Dalai Lama come to mind. Others, such as Hitler or Stalin, were consistent destroyers who tore others down at every opportunity. Most of us, of course, exist somewhere between these extremes. We have opportunities every day to work on heightening our awareness of our impact on others and the potential of that impact.

Most of us treasure stories of those who profoundly influenced our lives by some small word or action. For Paul it was a high school teacher, Mrs. Crum, who was somehow able to look past his previous disastrous performance in school. One day, seemingly out of nowhere, she asked him if he had ever thought about becoming a writer. Since he had barely passed English the year before, it struck Paul as a strange question. And yet that seed took root and now, half a dozen books and hundreds of articles later, Paul can now see himself through Mrs. Crum's eyes. For Steve, on the other hand, that pivotal moment came when his mother pointed out his skill and evident joy in working with children and suggested that perhaps he should consider becoming a teacher. Over the past several decades Steve has indeed enjoyed a rich career as teacher, school administrator, and district leader—and all of that grew out of his mother's loving suggestion. The power of those few words from Mrs. Crum and Mrs. Sokolow to leverage potential made them wise leaders. The powerful little secret is that we all have the potential to be wise leaders to each other.

Understanding the Powers of Two

The *powers of two* comes from the mathematical effect of multiplying the number two by itself and continuing that process until you have a vast number (2 x 2 x 2 x 2 x 2 …). For example, two to the second power is four, to the third power is eight, to the fourth sixteen, and so on. Two to the twentieth power, which is merely doubling two twenty times, is more than a million. If two people share an idea with two other people and each of them shares it with two more, in a short time the idea can reach thousands. The idea of paying things forward gets its strength from this concept as does the idea of random acts of kindness. A few people can have an enormous impact.

The popular notion that we should think globally but act locally is another aspect of this concept. Used by environmentalists to demonstrate that little acts at the local level can affect the entire world, it is also a way of affecting our spiritual and cultural environments. Since leadership is fundamentally about transformation, understanding that little acts can produce large effects can have tremendous influence in an organization. Empowerment is a way to create the effect of the *powers of two* in an organization. When a leader empowers a few and they empower a few and the empowerment is passed on, the organization flourishes.

Teaching Others to Fish

An old adage says that if I give you a fish you eat for a day, but if I teach you to fish you eat for a lifetime. This is a story of empowerment. Giving others the capacity to act and survive on their own empowers them to be independent and self-sufficient. Giving them the answers actually *dis*empowers them. When a new problem or challenge emerges, they will be waiting to see what you want them to do instead of knowing that they have the capacity to confront the challenge and overcome it. Teaching a person to fish— whether literally or metaphorically—provides knowledge that can be used over and over in different situations. The person who knows how to fish can decide where to fish, when to fish, and what kinds of and even how many fish to catch. *The ability to decide is the ultimate empowerment of others.*

The Taoists teach that you should lead in such a way that when the work is done people will say, "We did it ourselves." This can be a difficult concept for leaders who may desire the limelight and the credit. But the best leaders don't care who gets the credit if the job is done well. And the best way to ensure it will be done well is to allow people to do it themselves.

Empowering people is more than simply making the decision to do so. You have to have sufficient self-confidence that you are not threatened by the efforts of those whom you lead. You have to trust your staff to do what is best. You have to forgive their mistakes. You have to be patient if the task is not done at your speed.

Empowering leaders must be teachers. Not only do they have to see themselves in that way, but they need the skill of good teachers to allow the process of empowerment to unfold. Leadership is also "teacher-ship." Every interaction by a leader creates either dependence or independence. The leader/teacher strives to make the process one that leads to independence.

One fundamental question a leader must ask is "Who is the focus on?" If the focus is on the leader, people will feel they must please the leader rather than pleasing themselves. Constrained by their own expectations, they will feel disheartened because everything they do is for someone else. If the focus of the leader is on others, then those others will feel supported and enhanced in their work. One of the hardest lessons for a leader to understand is that power and influence are not diminished when they are given away—but rather increased and enhanced.

Making the Many One

While independence is critical in empowering an organization, there must also be a connection among all the independent parties. Our society is built from a social contract. It is not enough to have good skills if those skills do not include the ability to respect others and work with them. Our history is fraught with the negative lessons provided by those who had good personal skills but lacked any sense of community and social responsibility. From Watergate to the Wall Street meltdown, we have seen well-educated, skillful people lose their way because they failed to comprehend the social contract and the integrity that bind us together. *The interplay between the leader and the led is at its core a dance of mutuality.* Understanding the words of Martin Luther King Jr., which state that we are tied into a single garment of destiny and that what affects one directly affects all indirectly, is central to the success of an organization, a country, or a family.

As leaders strive to make people independent, it is also necessary to make them *understand* their interdependence. A powerful contributor to our mutual success is understanding that we are all working in interconnected systems and that our interconnectedness allows us to leverage our power and energy. In the Pledge of Allegiance, our forefathers got it exactly right. They told Americans that we need to seek both liberty (independence) and justice for all (interdependence). This balance between the individual and the group is key to success in any form. We need freedom as individuals, but that freedom must be leavened by a sense of social responsibility. Wise and empowering leaders teach people to pursue their possibilities and climb the mountains that confront them—but also to understand that they are part of an expedition, and their success is dependent on the success of others, *and* the trip is only successful if everyone gets up and back down the mountain safely.

A basic need here is to understand that the goals of the organization (choosing which mountain to climb) are best achieved through involving people in setting those goals. People who are doing something for someone else will comply. If they feel they are doing it for themselves, however, they will run through walls to make it happen. Once the goals are set, real empowerment comes by loosening the ties that bind people and letting them soar.

Allowing People to Surprise You

Once you have taught people to fish, their success will surprise you. Some of them might catch a whale! When you remove boundaries and limitations, anything becomes possible. We presume that someone taught Michelangelo how to draw, but he went on to surpass his teacher. All great artists had modest beginnings. Greatness in any field starts with mediocrity. But practice, encouragement, and further training build greatness. How many artists of Michelangelo's caliber may never have flourished because of someone else's constricting limitations? How would our world be altered if every one of us had a sense of unlimited potential? What kind of organization would you have if everyone in it felt empowered to do everything they were capable of achieving?

Once you teach people to fish you have to step back and *let* them fish. Knowing how to do something, absent the opportunity to do so, is as bad as never knowing how. Once our children learn to drive, eventually we have to hand them the car keys. Scary! They may know the fundamentals of driving, but their skills are still limited—and the world is a big, dangerous place. But they will never get past the fundamentals without taking the wheel on their own. Walking won't teach them to drive. As they gain experience we can become more confident in them and their abilities. But that confidence will never come if we don't let them try.

Leaders have to let people try and fail and then encourage them to try again. Wise leaders understand that the straightest path to success is often through failure. That perspective is also empowering for others who witness such acts. Being given permission to try and fail and try again might lead someone to exceed all expectations.

Leveraging Human Potential

When leaders allow others to create and make mistakes, and when they open up the organization to new ideas and new ways of doing things, those acts create conditions in which people grow. Capitalizing on what is actually happening in the organization rather than only on what the leader wants—this creates leverage. Once this process of opening an organization starts to build, the possibilities for growth and change become exponential. And growth can very well occur in many directions.

The author Richard Farson, in a discussion with Paul about exponential growth, observed that training makes people alike, but education makes them different. He also noted that leaders who merely train their people are not empowering them. But the leader who educates people creates growth in all directions. This unleashes the energy available and creates a much more powerful outcome.

Picture Einstein's concept of $E=mc^2$ which incorporates the power of two by squaring the speed of light. Wise leaders create light in their organization, which, when coupled with the people affected, unleashes powerful forces. When leaders let their own light shine and then work to let the light of others shine, the result is incredible energy.

Wise leaders understand that human potential is limitless. They merely unleash that power. To see people as expendable resources who are easily disposed of is to miss the potential of the power that can be created when people are viewed as precious and limitless in their abilities. Wise leaders invest themselves in bringing out the best in the people around them. Unwise leaders build walls around their people. Wise leaders build a floor for people to stand on and stairs that they can climb. Wise leaders move away from command and control to support, collaboration, and affiliation; in doing so, they empower others and make their entire organization stronger.

To become The Wise Leader:

- **Use your gifts to empower others.**
- **Uplift others.**
- **Understand the powers of two and of exponential thinking.**
- **Embrace the adage: Teach me to fish and I fish for a lifetime.**
- **Help others become independent.**
- **Appreciate and foster independence.**
- **Know that when you teach people and trust people you unleash their potential.**
- **Know that empowerment is the best way to leverage human capital and potential.**
- **Give people permission to be who they really are.**
- **Foster collaboration and affiliation.**
- **Remember that you have the power to enhance everyone's self-image.**
- **Move away from a command-and-control orientation to a service-and-support orientation.**

CHAPTER 10

The Wisdom of Synergy

Synergy is a scientific principle and a key component of systems thinking. Wise leaders are constantly alert for ways to create and use synergy in their organizations because it is an effective way to leverage power and energy. In this chapter we'll discuss how the whole may be greater than the sum of its parts, the use of dialogue to evoke our best thinking, the forging and fostering of partnerships and synergistic relationships, and ways of enhancing synergistic collaboration.

Let's start with a parable: a guy dies and goes before Saint Peter. Saint Peter tells him, "I have bad news and good news. The bad news is you just died. But the good news is we're having a blue-light special this week. You can choose where you'll spend eternity. We're going to show you heaven and hell and then let you choose where to go. First I'm going to take you to hell."

When they get to hell the guy sees a big ballroom with a pot of stew in the middle of the room, and it smells great. Everybody in the room is holding these long-handled spoons. They were able to dip the spoons in the stew, but they couldn't get the stew to their mouths. So they're starving and it's a terrible, miserable place.

Now Saint Peter and the guy go to heaven. Again there's a big ballroom with a pot of stew in the middle of the room. Everybody has a long-handled spoon, just like in hell, except here everybody is fat and sassy. The man doesn't understand what caused the difference. Saint Peter explains that in heaven people work together to do something they couldn't do by themselves. In heaven they learned to work together and feed each other.

Wise leaders work to create heaven right here on earth.

Synergy is one of the mechanisms for releasing potentiality between and among people. The energies of all the involved parties build on one another like logs in a fire. Picture a single log burning in a fireplace. Now set fire to a second log, but don't let it touch the first log, and then ignite a third log without letting it touch the first two. Look at the intensity of the flames, and the amount of heat and light being generated by those three logs burning separately. Now (using a pair of tongs, of course) move the first log so that it rests on the second and watch what happens to the flames, the heat, and the light. Finally, move the third burning log so that it rests on the other two, and observe the intensity of the flames, and the far greater amount of heat and light being produced. Clearly something different is taking place. The difference is synergy.

Creating and Using Synergy

Wise leaders create conditions that foster synergistic thinking and relationships. They provide opportunities for people to come together to plan, engage in dialogue, collaborate, and solve problems. They use a combination of standing and ad hoc teams and committees to bring people together. They foster open systems of communication and use technology to make it easy for people to network and share ideas. They create organizational structures to bring together people with diverse skills and perspectives.

But bringing people together physically or through technology is only the beginning. Team leaders need training in collaborative skills, team building, and facilitating team dynamics. Synergistic relationships work best in a climate of trust, openness, and safety, all of which flow from wise leadership.

When the conditions are right, synergistic thinking emerges spontaneously. In a synergistic environment people feel more creative and empowered. The effect can be transformative for individuals *and* the organization because everyone is bringing their best stuff to the table. Each person feels empowered to tap into his or her best thinking, which is then multiplied and amplified by the other members of the team. When the whole becomes greater than its parts, and each member of the team knows that he or she is an integral part of the whole, then good feelings—and greatly enhanced creativity—result.

The Whole May Be Greater Than the Sum of Its Parts

When we studied plane geometry in high school we learned that the whole equals the sum of its parts. Although this is true in plane geometry, in life—when the dynamic of synergy is at work—the whole is actually *greater* than the sum of its parts. The relationship between us (Paul and Steve) is synergistic. This book you're reading is beyond what Steve could create alone and beyond what Paul could create alone. Our combined thinking is not simply additive; it is more than just Steve's thoughts plus Paul's thoughts. Our interaction, which created this book, is synergistic.

We stimulate each other's thinking and, through the process of dialogue, something new emerges. Our energies not only combine, but due to the process of synergy, the total energy between us actually expands and multiplies.

Paul intuitively understood the power of synergy before he ever knew the word. As a young superintendent in Princeton, he carried out the following exercise. He divided his administrative team into several groups. Every team member was asked to read several paragraphs and then answer some questions as individuals. They then formed into teams. The teams had to agree on the answers to the questions. When the individual answers and the team answers were scored, in every instance the teams outscored the highest-scoring individual on the team. More heads were clearly better than one—a powerful example of the whole being greater than the sum of its parts. It's not simply an addition of $1 + 1 + 1 = 3$. It's $1 + 1 + 1 = 3+$. The collaborative process created something new. If you don't believe that, then you operate very differently as a leader—you don't work at bringing people together.

In fact, we know leaders who, as a part of their style, are divisive. They play people off of one another. They create conflict within the organization, calling it "creative conflict." In reality, however, that way of working creates dissension and friction within an organization. Such leaders subscribe to the Darwinian theory of leadership: let the fittest survive. We think they're missing something very important. You must look not only at the product of the synergistic interaction, but also at the effect on the individuals involved. In a synergistic organization the people themselves tend to buy into the work of the organization, the people themselves experience the benefits of the growth, the people themselves create connections that will be useful in other dynamics that have yet to occur, and the people themselves feel a sense of ownership and pride in what ultimately emerges from their combined efforts.

Synergy allows for surprise to take place. When you are working in a synergistic situation sometimes you come up with unexpected outcomes. Synergy is not a straight-line way of looking at the world. Taking new paths and new directions has the power to spark creativity. The interplay of the individuals allows for something new to emerge. Wise leaders understand that synergistic processes generate dynamic solutions in an ever-changing world.

Using Dialogue to Evoke Our Best Thinking

People often ask us how we collaborate on the books we write together, including this one. In a word—dialogue. Dialogue is an empowering form of discourse. On the surface it may look like conversation or a discussion, but a closer look reveals a dynamic, organic, almost alchemical process at work. For example, look at the subtitle of this section: "Using Dialogue to Evoke Our Best Thinking." In our actual dialogue we *reframed* the subtitle as a question: How can leaders use dialogue to evoke the best thinking in themselves and others? This is the Rosetta Stone of dialogue: change whatever you want to explore into a question.

Once you start with a question the process is evocative. Not only does our conscious mind become engaged when there's a question on the table, but when the conditions are right our unconscious mind becomes engaged as well. It's not just the particular question that we're contemplating—it's what you're saying about it that stimulates thought in me and vice versa. People know a great deal, but they don't always know *what* they know until they're placed in a circumstance where a probing question, or interesting perspective, or something partially shaped by another person comes into their sphere of consciousness. Then they will naturally build on that if they listen in an open way to what the other person is saying. Once the process is started, it seems as though the ideas begin to collaborate *through us* by themselves. They take on an energy or life of their own. We discovered that the process in which we engaged is a vivid example of synergy.

Earlier we shared an old joke where one guy says to the other guy, "Don't you think the two biggest problems in the world are ignorance and apathy?" The other guy says, "I don't know and I don't care." That perspective would stop dialogue in its tracks! Dialogue requires both knowing *and* caring. Dialogue is intellectual, in that you learn from the other person, but it includes a caring aspect that says, in effect, "I care enough about you to listen to what you have to say and to use my energy to interact with you."

Wise leaders know that one way to show people that you care is to listen to them. But dialogue goes beyond listening to *hearing*— hearing that incorporates a reflective process, so that the other person knows that they've been heard. This process is sometimes called "active listening," in which you use your own words to show you understand what the other person is saying before adding your thoughts to the dialogue. You can question a person and ask them to clarify or expand on something they've said. But avoid being confrontational or argumentative; that can stop the dialogue process cold, causing most people to narrow their focus and pull back their energy, rather than allowing it to flow naturally. Dialogue is an expansive and creative process in which thoughts can emerge in a free-flowing manner.

Another important element of dialogue is "wait time." You must be very patient in allowing the other person or persons to formulate their thoughts. If they sense patience on your part, they can be patient with themselves and allow their thoughts to emerge. If they sense that they're talking to someone who is very impatient and who does not allow open space in the dialogue, then what often happens is that they throw out quick answers to move the process forward—but their responses lack depth. They will say something appropriate, but something deeper might have come out, if only the other person had exercised greater patience. Wait time shows both caring and respect.

To this point we've been discussing dialogue in a way that focuses on the interaction between two people, but Joseph Jaworski in his book *Synchronicity* and James Redfield in *The Celestine Prophecy* talk about dialogue from a group perspective as well. One of the images that their work brings to mind is a group of people sitting around a table in a meeting. When one person in the group is ready to contribute to the dialogue, then everyone's attention focuses on that individual. The attention of the other members of the group creates a group energy field that helps stimulate and energize the person who is the object of their focus in a way that helps him or her contribute to the dynamic exchange that is unfolding through dialogue.

For example, a person in the group thought he was going to say A, but by being the focus of the others' attention, he feels important enough to say more than A. He says A and B. And once he says A and B, other people might contribute C and D. Therefore, instead of getting A alone, you've already advanced four or five letters in the alphabet! You've already reaped a richer outcome than would have resulted without focusing the group's attention and valuing the contributing group member. The result: a synergism that tends to evoke the best thinking in the person who is in focus and also in the entire group.

Forging and Fostering Partnerships

Early in life we're taught by our parents to share our toys and play nicely with others. We start out being self-centered and territorial but gradually learn to share; we learn that playing with others is more fun than playing alone. We are social beings who learn about ourselves and others by interacting in countless social interactions.

But something even more dynamic unfolds in our interactions with others that is captured in the wisdom of John Donne's famous line, "No man is an island." Somehow, whole as any one of us may be in and of ourselves, we are incomplete. One of the ways in which we complete ourselves is by forging partnerships throughout our lives. These partnerships may take the form of play groups or friendships; later they take the form of relationships, life partners, and work groups, because ultimately we can't be who we really are in isolation. We have a need to be in community and in connection with others, and partnerships are the vehicle by which we reach out to others and others reach out to us so that we can come together into a greater whole.

In some important ways we don't know what we look like without looking in the mirror. And to some extent other people are our mirrors. Through other people the world reflects back to us who we are and what we are. Part of the dynamic of partnering leads to a deeper understanding of ourselves. Wise leaders know that they can expand their creativity by interacting with others, and move their ideas forward by partnering and co-creating with others. They also know that ultimately, if they don't learn how to forge and foster partnerships, they have no one to lead.

Fostering Synergistic Relationships

Wise leaders work at building relationships. They reach out to others in a spirit of trust and openness. One way of showing openness is through self-disclosure. As humans, by sharing our vulnerability and human frailties with others, we can build relationships and create connections with others. Sharing our vulnerability can also engender trust because we trust others with knowing our frailties and with knowing we're aware that we are less than perfect, like them.

Another powerful dynamic for fostering synergistic relationships is caring. When people know that you care about them and the work they are doing, they invest more energy in the relationship, thus increasing the opportunity for synergy. It's also important to have a leadership style that shows that you really value synergistic relationships. If you value such relationships, you are more likely to use approaches and create conditions that will foster them. For example, as the leader you play a key role in determining how and in what ways people will be brought together and for what purposes. You play a central role in determining which people will be called to work together and in creating the climate and guidelines for various types of work groups and committees. Will you put together people who tend to be more like-minded or who represent greater diversity of thought? How much time will you give people to form synergistic relationships? As a leader you can simply say you believe in synergy, or you can model it by creating collaborative groups that are not just for show and by giving people the time and resources that allow synergistic relationships to bear fruit. Enthusiasm is a good catalyst for synergy. Emotions are contagious. When leaders show enthusiasm, a positive infection is created and people respond accordingly.

You can also foster synergistic relationships by conveying to the members of a group that you really believe in the power that resides in the group to solve particular problems and to generate creative solutions. Such expressions cannot be merely a facade. You must believe sincerely in what you say, acknowledging that you have selected them as a special group of people and that you are confident that they are going to generate interesting, creative solutions to the problem or task at hand. You are thus conveying the confidence, the belief, and the trust that you, as their leader, have not just for them as individuals, but also for them as a vitally important group.

Our task as leaders is to convey this message (or something like it): "I know each of you. I chose you because you have unique skills and qualities to bring to this work group (or committee or task force). This task force is charged with an important responsibility. I know you are going to rise to the challenge. I'm going to support you as needed throughout the process." You are explicitly tasking the work group with its mission or charge and letting them know that you are prepared to allocate whatever resources are needed to allow the synergistic process to unfold.

The group chairperson plays an important role in the synergistic process. Group members need to feel safe, respected, and valued. The process needs to be expansive rather than constrained. If each member can speak freely and share his thinking without being rushed or hushed, he is more likely to bring his best thinking to the task at hand. People need to be given time to generate divergent perspectives, time to mull things over, time to reflect, and time to build on each other's contributions. Synergy unfolds when there is trust, mutual respect, and a sense of purpose.

Using Group Energy to Enhance Synergistic Collaboration

Wise leaders are sensitive to the collective energy of the groups they lead. As a leader you are in a position to set the feeling tone of the group. We have found that a positive feeling tone enhances the process of synergistic collaboration. How do you foster positive feelings, which then are reflected in the group's collective energy? You try to create a space for people to blend into the group dynamic. We advocate using humor to help people move into a comfortable place of being with one another. You can also diminish conflict by using humor to minimize tension. What you are trying to do is lower the walls that everyone carries with them. You want to get the walls down so nothing stands between the people in the group, which then creates a sense of "groupness." To nurture real synergy, which is expansive, you need a group dynamic that allows people to feel valued, trusted, and safe.

Picture a think tank or brainstorming situation in which no idea is too foolish to be considered. Even though an idea may be way out of the box, we post it on the board anyway and give it its due because it occurred to a member of the group. By making sure that everyone's ideas are given due consideration, you show that every member of the group is valued. The leader's role is to set a tone that establishes that the entire group is interested in each person's contribution, that we're going to ensure that everybody is heard fully, and that we're not going to rush to a decision until there has been a thorough airing of all possibilities.

The proper tone promotes collaboration and consensus building. It's one thing to say that everyone in the group should feel respected, but what happens when one group member starts putting another down? If we allow that to happen, then the system inevitably starts to close. Whether it's by the action of the leader or by the collective leadership of the group members, responsibility must be taken for creating an open process that allows everyone to feel valued, because only by creating an open process and an open-feeling tone in the group can the process become truly synergistic.

To get a sense of a synergistic dynamic, picture the following possible scenarios: we've been in groups in which everyone is supposed to work together and then appoint one person to report the group's conclusions. Several things can go wrong here. There may be one dominant person in the group who wants to force his or her ideas onto the entire group, which usually kills any discussion. Another possible scenario is that the group enjoys a pretty good discussion, but the person doing the reporting reports only his or her own ideas.

Instead, envision a group whose members truly build on each other's ideas. One person throws out something good and somebody else grabs it and says "Great, wow, what if we added to that?" and a third person says "Right, we could add this too!"—and real excitement begins to be generated and a powerful energy created. Then, if the person reporting on the whole discussion truly captures the excitement and the ideas, even greater excitement can build, as well as a feeling of consensus. Members of the group can honestly say, "That really worked! We really *were* heard! My ideas are up there! We created something new with each other!"

This kind of synergistic experience can be incredibly heady. It's euphoric and almost narcotic in its effect when a group is building something new together in a way that is both powerful and empowering. Wise leaders understand the power of this synergistic dynamic and how to foster it.

To become The Wise Leader:

- Use the power of synergy.
- Be aware that the whole can be greater than the sum of its parts.
- Use dialogue to evoke the best thinking in yourself and others.
- Seek to forge and foster partnerships.
- Foster synergistic relationships.
- Use shared group energy to enhance synergistic collaboration.
- Bring forces and folks together.
- Release potentiality in others.
- Care about others.
- Know that synergy fosters creativity and renewal.

Part III

CHAPTER 11

The Wisdom of Paying Attention

Paul, who grew up in rural West Virginia, used an old joke to describe his impoverished childhood. He liked to say that he was so poor that he couldn't pay attention in school. The sad reality, though, is that the inability to pay attention impoverishes the spirit and weakens a leader. Wisdom does not come only from inside a person. Wisdom also comes from outside, and you let it in by paying attention. *Attention grounds you in the here and now.* Attention allows the leader to focus. The most important decision a leader can make is deciding what to focus his or her attention on. The leader's attention signals to others what is important and what they should attend to. A lack of attention, on the other hand, calls to mind the absent-minded professor who is brilliant in thought but ignorant in action.

Both Steve and Paul lived in or around Princeton, New Jersey, for several years. Princeton's most famous resident was probably Albert Einstein, who spent the last decades of his life in Princeton working at the Institute for Advanced Study—a rarefied campus created as a home for great thinkers. Einstein lived about a mile from the Princeton campus. He walked to and from work every day, often walking home for lunch. Many days, the story goes, he would walk the mile home at midday, reach his front porch, and forget why he had come home. He would then turn around and walk back to the Institute, no doubt continuing to think great thoughts, but on an empty stomach. Here was one of the greatest minds who ever lived—the genius of the twentieth century—who was too preoccupied with thought to tend to his own physical needs. He lacked attention on the here and now. No doubt he could focus unparalleled attention on thoughts and theories, but he lacked the ability to take in the world around him—the epitome of the absent-minded professor.

Attention must be paid to both the foreground and the background. It is necessary to focus both on the immediate problems or issues at hand, and also to be aware of the world surrounding the problem. A solution that fails to take the context into consideration will be incomplete.

The leader's perspective can dictate what he or she sees. How something appears depends on the lens that is used. If you choose a close-up lens your focus will be on the small (or the immediate), while a wide-angled lens takes in the broader context and examines objects from a distance. A wise leader is forever shifting lenses so that both the near and now, as well as the far and future, are given due consideration.

Leaders must also understand that what they choose to focus on makes a statement about who they are and what their values are. The Bible tells us that "where your treasure is, there your heart will be also." What you treasure dictates where you put your heart and soul. When others are watching you lead, where you put your attention tells them all they need to know about what you value and what really drives you. Where your attention is, there is your spirit also.

Wise Leaders Pay Attention to What Is Important

One of the greatest challenges a leader faces is to attend closely to what is important. The world conspires against that kind of focused attention. In a world where the urgent seems always to trump the important, it is difficult for a leader to stay focused on what is most important. Day-to-day petty pressures intrude on long-term, more important issues. A leader can begin to feel like a rat on a wheel— running furiously but getting nowhere. If you allow yourself to become bogged down in the trivial you'll find it difficult to attain the sublime. Priorities are not about what we plan to do at ten o'clock tomorrow. Instead, they involve knowing how what you do at ten has to do with your life.

Two of the most valuable skills a leader needs are the ability to analyze the past so it can serve as a guide, and also the ability to plan for the future. If that is all a leader does, however, he misses the present—where things really are happening. Paul once had a friend who was proud of saying that he was so focused on the future that the only thing he did in the present was breathe. He missed the point of leadership. The heart of leadership is in the present—in the moment. It is important to know *where* you are leading and to keep that ever in mind, but the work of leadership takes place in the now. The great irony of what Paul's friend said is that he died of a severe asthma attack that kept him from breathing. He forgot to do the one thing necessary to move from the present to the future!

Maintaining a focus on what is important is not easy. In their work as school leaders, both Paul and Steve saw countless kindergarten teachers go home at the end of every day with handprints and smudges all along the bottom of their dresses. Why? Because all day, every day, little hands were pulling at them, calling out "me, me, me."

There is the challenge facing leaders. Everyone around them needs their assistance and attention, and that can be a powerful distraction from staying focused on what is important.

The very environment in which we live is distracting. The pull of personal media and the fragmented way images bombard us via movies and television distracts us from paying attention to what is important, or even from relaxing and recentering ourselves. It's surprising that *everyone* doesn't suffer from attention deficit disorder! The world has become a white-water experience, with rapids waiting around every bend. Yet in the midst of that ever-present frenzy, the challenge for leaders is to keep attending to the things that count.

One of the secrets a wise leader understands is that sometimes the best way to move forward is by stepping back. Instead of plowing ahead into the next crisis, the wise leader takes a moment to stop and reflect on how all that is happening fits into a broader picture—and then steps forward again. The ancient Eastern practice of Taoism can be described as advising, "Don't just do something; stand there." That notion of intentional inaction is worth considering; it opens a space between actions that allows the doing to mean something and permits clarity to emerge.

For a leader to truly be wise, he or she must be able to get out of the box—to find alternative and divergent solutions to problems. And paying attention is the first step in that process. When the forces of the urgent conspire to move you forward, it's easy to ignore alternative solutions and answers. If the leader can shift the lens and consider different angles, a better solution is likely to arise. *This ability to consider alternatives is the essence of creative leadership.* Problems are not two-dimensional like a painting; they are three-dimensional like a sculpture. It is important to walk around and look at all sides of a problem. *That* is paying attention.

Attention in Thinking

As a man thinks, we are told, so shall he be. Every action starts with a thought. Parents will often scold a child who has done something wrong by asking, "What were you thinking?" Or as Bill Cosby once asked one of his children, "Was your head with you all day?" We adults often do many things that indicate we left our heads at home.

In reality, we have choices in what we think about. What we fill our heads with takes us along a certain path. Thought emits energy. If we think about something bad happening, we make that something more likely to happen. After her husband fell to his death, the wife of the great Karl Wallenda, tightrope walker and patriarch of the famous Flying Wallendas, said that final walk was the only one before which he had talked constantly about "not falling." Previously, he had always talked about succeeding. The thought of failure in his head led to disastrous failure. Certainly merely thinking something doesn't make it so, but it is a good start.

Thought is also the way we tap into our higher selves. For those with spiritual beliefs, it is one way we speak to the Infinite. You can't use Western Union or e-mail for that. You can't text the Infinite. You focus your attention and think it.

Attention in Doing

Have you ever walked into something that you knew was there? Paul once broke his toe on his bed, which had been sitting in the same place for years. He simply wasn't paying attention. Accidents are really testaments to inattention. Losing a sense of presence is the fastest way to break something. The people we are leading are constantly watching us to see if we lose our sense of presence. Expect them to do as you do, not as you say. If you lose your sense of attention and presence, so will they.

Modern society seems to value doing over thinking. (Compare an athlete's salary to a scientist's salary.) Yet doing without thinking is the ultimate act of stupidity. The mental plane and the physical plane cannot be separated safely. And don't overlook the spiritual plane, because it certainly seems to be connected to the other two planes. A wise leader understands and values all three planes and their connections and interconnections.

Attention in Being

Just as being mindless (and thoughtless) is dangerous, so is being disconnected from our higher self. When we fail to attend to our core values, our sense of purpose, our sense of our impact on others, we have failed to pay attention to our very being. In doing so, we have in the process become disconnected from our higher self.

It's possible to have a sense of purpose, but to have adopted the *wrong* purpose. Purpose focused only on yourself and your desires is ultimately destructive. A leader who has such a purpose is dangerous, and certainly not wise. Each of us needs to use our personal GPS to allow us to be guided in the ways we should be. You can be an effective leader without being connected to the deeper sense of purpose—but you can never be a wise one.

Although it's important to pay attention to our being, we must understand that our being is animated by our paying attention. The two are interconnected. Paul loves the desert; he finds a connection to nature there that's important to him—the plants, the animals, the smells, the views. The desert tends to change him into a mellower person because it's a place that connects him and grounds him.

He once asked a friend who knew him in different settings, "Am I different in the desert?"

She answered, "No, you are more you." That is the essence of connecting attention to being. When you really pay attention and have a sense of mindfulness, you are feeding the part of yourself that is the real you.

Maximizing Our Time on Task

The essence of efficient management is maximizing time on task, and the way to do that is by prioritizing. But just as we need to prioritize our days, we need to prioritize our lives. Some people seem to get more out of life; these folks prioritize their purpose.

Some people live in the same manner that we are told we should drink wine. They savor life. They look at its color, smell the bouquet, swirl it around to give it oxygen, and allow it to wash over them just as a good wine rolls over the tongue. Wise people understand what is important and what isn't. As the saying goes, when people are dying, rarely do they say they wish they had spent more time at work. Their regrets tend to center on not taking in life more fully, and on connecting more completely with others.

When Paul's mother was dying, he spent a lot of time with her. He missed a great deal of work. She apologized to him for complicating his already complicated life. He told her, "Mother, this time is my gift to you." Just as important, though, that time was also a gift to him. Being in that hospital room, just being there for her when a thousand things were calling for his attention, allowed him to know that being in her room doing nothing was the most important thing he could do. Just being in that moment was critical. It made him a better person because his *being* had paid attention to what was important.

Focusing Our Energy

The issue here is not only focusing our own energy but also helping those we depend upon, and who depend on us, to focus their energy. This leads to the concept of simplicity. Leaders and organizations tend to have multiple goals and priorities. Planning and goal-setting involve getting things done that are important to the organization, of course, but they often involve dealing with the unexpected. Sometimes events we didn't plan for become a top priority. In 2010, for example, President Obama was dealing with a troublesome economy, two wars, a recalcitrant Congress, political opposition, the need for health care, and Wall Street reform. Then along came the oil spill in the Gulf of Mexico, which shifted all the other existing priorities. How does a leader deal with such urgent and unexpected situations?

One answer is to simplify. Leaders have to be able to strip away the extraneous and get to the core. Cutting away distractions and getting to the real essence of things is key. The power of any great leader is to simplify the message and then stay focused on it. Jesus may have been divine, depending on your beliefs, but there is little doubt that he was a great teacher because he was able to simplify his message. He used parables and stories to focus people on the message.

Many leaders can become so caught up in initiatives and projects that those in the organization are lost. As some have pointed out, the main thing is to keep the main thing the main thing. The larger the organization, the simpler the messages must be so people will not get lost.

Attention Draws Others' Attention

Attention acts as a magnet to others. When the leader can focus on what is important, everyone else is better able to focus. This sense of focus leads to commitment and action. A sense of commitment is attractive to others. They want to be part of the action.

Leaders are role models by choice or circumstance. In childhood we learn to play "follow the leader," and that carries over into adult life. Leaders can magnetize and galvanize others. They draw them together and get them to act. The more people who are drawn to the action, the more people who will be drawn. Attention of this sort produces a multiplier effect.

Leaders who are able to create attention do so out of a sense of certainty. If the leader is clear on what needs to be done, others will follow. We have all been in situations where no one really knows where he is going; if one person acts with certainty, however, others will follow them. Paul has an unusually good sense of direction. He can go into towns halfway around the world where he has never been and be able to find his way around. Others will begin to follow him. Some will ask him, "Are you sure you know where you're going?" He always answers affirmatively, and off they go. People follow his sense of certainty. Occasionally, it must be said, he really *doesn't* know where he's going and leads his comrades down a blind alley. Well, leaders aren't always right, but they have to be willing to lead.

Of course, it's quite possible for leaders to have a sense of passion and certainty but not be the sort of person others should follow. Here Hitler and Osama bin Laden come to mind. The difference lies in the arena of moral purpose. Wise leaders have a sense of moral purpose whose center is the welfare of others. Destructive leaders tend to have agendas that are about themselves. Wise leaders turn lights on and uplift others; destructive leaders dim the lights of others and hold them down.

How to Keep Your Focus

We place blinders on horses and donkeys to keep them focused, but that is no way to lead human beings. Leaders need to look forward to what is possible, but they also need to be aware of what is happening around them. This kind of far-flung awareness allows thoughtfulness to play a part.

Being proactive, not reactive, is vitally important. Overcoming a sense of drift and inertia takes effort, and effort can be necessary to stay focused on what is important. Being forced to react to others' agendas causes some of any leader's most frustrating times. When you are following your own agenda, your energy level is higher and you feel able to move mountains. One person's action can become another's distraction, however. Paul and Steve, as career educators, often found that a school board's purpose can become a superintendent's distraction. A superintendent's edict can become a teacher's frustration. A teacher's assignment can become a student's cause to mentally drift off.

How does a leader move forward and persuade others to follow? Empowering others is a key. If people feel that they have a say and a role in the process, they can become excited quite easily. Leaders can set the goal, but they need to negotiate the process with those who will be carrying it out.

Using Images, Signs, and Symbols

Wise leaders use the power of image, story, and metaphor to engage others and bring them along. Signs and symbols are shortcuts to the psyche. Politicians, for instance, have used the flag as a shortcut to appeal to people's sense of national identity. The flag is an enormously powerful image that embodies emotions and beliefs in one visible symbol.

Effective leaders know that emotions are as critical as intellect in moving people. The power of metaphor is that it connects an intellectual concept to an emotional feeling. Metaphors are word pictures. A picture is worth a thousand words (or many more), which is why political leaders are always using "photo ops" to get their message across.

Several years ago the president of the United States visited the Allied cemetery at Normandy, and many photos showed him walking among the crosses there. Since the president's so-called political "base" was Christian, he used that handy historic symbol as a means of connecting with them. Normandy as a location ties into our nation's deepest sense of history, patriotism, and sacrifice. The president was attempting to connect the war he was leading with a more universally accepted war of an earlier time. The many pictures and videos showed the president walking alone, not surrounded by

Secret Service or staff members. Even though hundreds of others were standing just out of the picture, the image of him alone among the graves was a powerful one.

While we recognize that political leaders are extremely adept at this kind of messaging, leadership is leadership, and any leader must learn to use the sense of symbol and image to help others focus attention on what is important.

Leadership is a reciprocal act. You follow in order to lead. You pay attention to others so they will pay attention to you. Before all, however, you need to pay attention to your values, your thoughts, and then your actions. You have to take in the world around you so that you can change it for the better.

To become The Wise Leader:

- **Understand the key role attention plays in leadership.**
- **Focus your attention through thought.**
- **Focus your attention through action.**
- **Focus your attention through being.**
- **Know how to use your time effectively.**
- **Focus power and energy on important issues and initiatives.**
- **Know that attention is a magnet for attracting others.**
- **Pay attention to see that attention is paid.**
- **Keep your focus.**
- **Minimize distractions.**
- **Use images, signs, and symbols to communicate and create common purpose.**

CHAPTER 12

The Wisdom of Having an Attitude of Gratitude

Gratitude is a powerful force. Many wise leaders have embraced the catchy phrase: "Have an attitude of gratitude." It's certainly debatable that you can't be too rich or too thin, but we maintain that you cannot be too grateful.

Wise leaders truly do have an attitude of gratitude. They are grateful to the people around them and to life itself for the countless gifts that have been given to them. They show their gratitude in many ways, both internally and externally. Gratitude is one of the several principles of Wise Leadership that is contagious. Gratitude begets gratitude. The objects of our gratitude are boundless: our families, our friends, our colleagues, our opportunities, our careers, our lessons, our gifts, our good fortune, our good health, nature, life itself, and the divine.

Gratitude isn't just a feeling—it's a form of energy. The energy of gratitude has the power to attract and empower. We know that when we appreciate others, they are more likely to appreciate us, and similarly, when we appreciate the unique gifts of others, they are more likely to appreciate *our* unique gifts. Gratitude and appreciation are among those special attributes that can never be used up. Give gratitude away and you still have it. Wise leaders seem to abound with gratitude for so many things, but especially for the honor of serving others.

Gratitude is not only a powerful principle of wise leadership but also an expression of love and connection between people and the world, and between human beings and the divine. The well from which gratitude springs is limitless, as are the opportunities for each of us to express it. The more grateful you are, the more grateful you become. The more gratitude you express, the more gratitude you receive. Genuine gratitude is empowering. It empowers you and those you lead. You are hard-wired with the capacity to both receive and express gratitude. As leaders, you can embody this principle and magnify its positive effects in the world.

Having an Attitude of Gratitude

People often view gratitude too narrowly: as something you feel when someone does something good for you—being grateful for a favor or a gift, for example. The attitude of gratitude, as we see it, is much broader than that. It's a way of looking at life that accepts and is grateful for whatever life brings you—good, bad, or ugly. An attitude of gratitude transcends the specific interchange that might be taking place; it is not simply "I'm grateful for the gift" or "I'm grateful for the favor," but "I'm also grateful for the hurt" or "I'm grateful for the negative lesson that you brought me" or "I'm grateful for this difficult period that I'm experiencing because it will help me learn or grow or become stronger." Having an attitude of gratitude is an approach to life that embraces whatever may come.

In life, new ideas and understandings arrive at different times and in different forms. The whole concept of having an attitude of gratitude is something Steve took into his heart instantly; it became a part of him and his expanded worldview. An attitude of gratitude is one of the lenses that is available to you always, not just at specific times.

Sometimes you may need to remind yourself gently when that attitude is eluding you. When you are down or things aren't going well, gratitude may seem counterintuitive, but it is vitally needed at such times. When you look at everything through grateful eyes, you will always see events, people, and experiences for which to be grateful. To help remember this, you might consider creating a small sign that says: "Have an attitude of gratitude."

A time when we're especially mindful of our attitude of gratitude is when we engage in prayer. When Paul prays, he always says his prayers of gratitude first. Expressing gratitude for the good things is easy, but expressing gratitude for the bad things is not. Paul believes that even the difficulties and hurts he experiences can help him in some way. He tries to accept the good and the bad with the same attitude, and his mind-set reflects a pervasive attitude of gratitude.

Steve also starts his prayers with expressions of gratitude, but his approach is different. He routinely expresses gratitude for his blessings: family, friends, home, health, education, career, opportunities for service, and so forth. Then he adds an open-ended prayer of gratitude for whatever is happening in his life now: a new friend, the return to health of someone close, a new career opportunity, the birth of a granddaughter, the achievement of a goal, a lesson learned—whatever shows up. Committing his heart and mind to an attitude of gratitude allows Steve to experience life in a new way. Regardless of what he is doing, or thinking, or feeling as he experiences life, there's an additional dimension that opens when he remembers to be appreciative and grateful for what is unfolding. It's as though the experience acquires a greater richness from life that simply does not happen if you don't have that additional dimension: life's spiritual underpinning.

Wise Leaders Are Mindful of Life's Blessings

Why is it important for us to be mindful of life's blessings? First of all, blessings are the dessert—the syrup on the top of the ice-cream sundae, the cherry on top of the syrup. Blessings are the bonuses, the things that add extra depth to life. If you don't pay attention to your blessings you're left with a gray picture without the sense of vibrancy provided by the blessings.

Part of a leader's role is modeling. If you, the leader, are not mindful of blessings, then how will anybody else in the organization be fully aware of them? How do you measure progress in an organization? One way to view progress is as a measurement of blessings, of moving from one blessing to the next. If you don't have a sense of that progression, then you can't appreciate where you've been. An attitude of gratitude is a way of creating signposts to show how well you're doing and to create a sense of the richness in the life you're living.

Wise Leaders Show Gratitude for Help and Support

When you show gratitude for the help and support you receive, the impact only multiplies—the good stuff just keeps coming.

Gratitude creates plentitude—you end up with more. When you are not grateful you typically end up with less. Lacking gratitude, even those who have much may experience life as empty and sterile because they don't appreciate what they have. Gratitude is a magic word—the "open sesame" of life. When you know how to be grateful and can express gratitude in appropriate terms, the rock rolls away and the treasure is revealed.

Gratitude begets gratitude. Its expression attracts similar energy in others and in the universe, so that the very act of expressing gratitude sends out an energy field that not only comes back but also is magnified. Think of sprinkling Miracle-Gro® in the garden of life. Gratitude has the effect of almost magically creating abundance; sprinkle it about and watch everything grow.

People often tell little children that the magic words are "please" and "thank you." Guess what? Those are still magic words even when you grow up! Saying "thank you" is expressing gratitude. How many notes do you write to people expressing your gratitude? Do you appreciate how important those notes are to people? The words are important. You may *say* "thank you," but if you take the next step and put the words in writing they are even more powerful. You can use e-mail or print a letter from your computer, but the message will mean more if you write a note or letter by hand. Handwriting seems so much stronger than electronic communication because it is more personal.

Paul frequently receives notes and letters about speeches he has given or articles he has written. When he gets thank-you notes or e-mails from people, it makes him want to do more, which is part of the Miracle-Gro® effect. Gratitude reinforces whatever good things you are doing. You want to do more when you know that what you're doing is appreciated and valued. It's not so much that you're looking for a pat on the back; rather, it's good to be told that your energy and effort have meaning for others. Knowing that, you want to do even more. It's a way of refueling the engine.

Wise Leaders Are Grateful for Progress

All of life is incremental. Leaders should seek to create transformation, understanding that true transformation, like most change and improvement, comes incrementally. At one level, we can be grateful for a sense of progress because that's our measure of where we've been and how far we have left to go. Measuring progress helps us know how we're doing. When you get frustrated at work, take a moment to examine how far you've come. Instead of constantly looking ahead and talking only about where you and your organization have not yet gone and how far you still have to go, turn around for a second and appreciate the distance you've come from where you started. When you do that, you tend to feel better about yourself, which then empowers you to tackle what lies ahead. It's so easy to take the progress you've made for granted. But being reminded of a previous baseline and how far you've come from that point helps you (and those for whom you're responsible) see that you can progress that far again from today's baseline.

At one time, Paul's board members lacked an awareness and appreciation of where they'd come from as an organization; instead, they were focusing on their current frustrations. Paul revived an old practice—he made a chart that compared where the organization was financially when he arrived and where they were currently. The difference was dramatic. Paul realized that his board didn't appreciate the organization's progress because members simply didn't have baseline information.

Organizations and the people in them can change rapidly, and maintaining an institutional memory can become more and more difficult. To create an attitude of gratitude about progress, leaders need to benchmark progress from a historical perspective—ignoring those who say, "I only care about where we are today" or "What have you done for me lately?"

In his writing, Terry Deal, former professor at the University of Southern California, emphasizes the importance of celebration. Deal maintains that organizations should celebrate milestones and steps of progress because doing so empowers members to move forward. Celebrations provide a sense of achievement and completion and satisfaction that you have accomplished something, even as you recognize that there is still more to do. In many organizations—and education is a particularly notorious example—leaders do very little celebrating; as a profession, educators tend to be overly modest. Somehow educators feel that it's inappropriate to draw attention to themselves, or they don't take credit for what others expected them to do—as though accomplishing the enormously daunting task of educating the nation's children were no big deal.

Some people have this unfortunate attitude: "You get paid to do a job, so do your job and get your paycheck. That's the social contract we have." This narrow view does not unleash human potential because, though everyone wants to earn a living, that's not the core value explaining why people work—and nowhere is this more true than in the field of education. People are hard-wired to want to make a difference. They want to see progress in their own growth and evolution, as well as progress in their organization's growth and evolution. That's what people need to feel valued and gratified.

Progress is essential because if things are not living and growing, they're deteriorating and dying. Progress is not only about moving forward—it's about growing and evolving. Leaders have the power and the responsibility to help people understand this.

Wise Leaders Are Grateful for Obstacles and Adversaries

We subscribe to Nietzsche's reflection: "That which does not kill us makes us stronger." Most of Paul's greatest progress has come as a result of obstacles, adversity, and adversaries, from those times when he experienced pain or learned a tough lesson. Many times growth seems to be prompted more as a result of bad lessons than good lessons. People tend to take the good stuff in their lives for granted, whereas the bad stuff makes them stop and pay attention. When good things come our way we tend to move on with our lives, continuing in the same direction without too much reflection. When things are going badly, sooner or later we tend to stop and try to figure out what needs to be changed or added or subtracted that will improve the situation.

Paul is proud of the people who are his enemies, and he has tried to choose them well. He exercises as much care in choosing his enemies as he does in choosing his friends because he believes that both our friends and our enemies say much about who we are and what we stand for. He believes that if he didn't oppose some people, he would have cause to worry about himself. Understand that Paul is not advocating that you go out of your way to create enemies—though some people do just that, alienating everyone around them. But it's a good thing if some people oppose you and what you stand for.

Paul recalls a White House event at which a woman said some negative things about him. He smiled, thinking, "If you don't like what I'm saying and doing, I'm probably hitting the right notes." Such encounters can define who you are in an appropriate way, and you should be grateful for the clarification. In addition, they make you stronger, and they can give you lessons that allow you to redo or rethink something—you're not *always* right, after all. When someone opposes you, it might be because you're wrong, so opposition can give you an opportunity to pause and reflect, which is a useful tool for leaders. After reflection, sometimes you may decide that you are indeed moving in the right direction, and the show of opposition merely reinforces your commitment to that direction. At other times you may say to yourself, "There's an interesting point here that I had not considered. I'd better regroup and see what I need to modify and do differently."

Wise Leaders Show Gratitude for Love Received

One way to show your gratitude for love received is by being more loving yourself. A song by the Beatles includes the line "In the end, the love you take is equal to the love you make." We show our gratitude for love, in part, by loving back. Becoming a more loving person is a powerful way of expressing gratitude for the love that you've received. This doesn't mean simply talking more about love; it means acting in more loving ways—treating *love* as a verb. Another way to show gratitude for the love you receive is by trying to be a better person. For some people, being loved smooths their rough edges and rounds them out. In the movie *As Good as It Gets*, the character played by Jack Nicholson tells his girlfriend, "You make me want to be a better man."

With a broad view of love, which is the ultimate form of caring, you recognize just how much and how often love comes your way. It comes not only *in* many different forms, but also *through* many different forms: from coworkers and colleagues as well as family or friends, from our pets, from divine sources, and, one could argue, sometimes even from life itself. This larger view gives you a bigger arena in which to show your gratitude.

Wise Leaders Are Grateful for Love Accepted

Some people are quite comfortable in the act of giving love: they are caring people who give freely of themselves in a loving way to the people around them and the environments in which they live. But the very same people may have a great deal of trouble accepting love that comes their way. Often these folks are made acutely uncomfortable by others' expressions of love and gratitude to them; they may disregard such gestures or shrug them off as unnecessary. We believe that many people find it much harder to accept expressions of love than to give love.

For leaders, it is especially important to be open to expressions of love that come their way. In respect to love, it may actually be more blessed to receive than to give because, ultimately, it is only by receiving love that we have it to give. If you can't accept love, it becomes much harder, if not impossible, to give it. If you're open to receiving love, it's just like gratitude: the more you get, the more you have to give, and the more you want to give.

One reason many people find it hard to receive or accept love may be that they feel somehow unworthy. Groucho Marx once said, "I don't care to belong to any club that will have me as a member."

In other words, how could I possibly accept your love, since I'm not worthy of being loved? Many people are just plain uncomfortable with love. They don't know how to handle the gift of love with grace. Although the inability to accept love may be quite common, such an inability poses a special problem for leaders. Almost by definition, you may receive love from those whom you lead. If you can't be grateful for that love and accept it, your ability to lead may be restricted because you don't reciprocate appropriately.

Being able to show gratitude for love received presumes that you're willing to acknowledge receiving it, and many people are simply unable to do so. Some may be afraid to show that they like receiving love because they might become dependent on it, and then how can you be sure that love will be there when you want or need it?

On a more positive note, accepting love also empowers the giver. If you accept the love that others bestow on you, and they can see your acceptance of their gift, they become empowered by their giving. Acceptance itself is a gift. This may be a helpful perspective, especially for men, as men seem to find it more difficult to give and receive love in a demonstrable way; in Western society, men have been acculturated not to show their feelings.

Love is a powerful force. Organizations would be healthier if their leaders could become more comfortable in both accepting and giving love. Will our culture ever reach a stage that allows men to demonstrate love and still be considered manly? We hope so, but it may be difficult to achieve. Some women leaders, depending on their background, may shy away from accepting or showing love in a work environment for fear of being perceived as too feminine or too soft. We would argue that leaders need to be able to accept love and give it, regardless of their gender.

Wise Leaders Are Grateful for the Opportunity to Help Others

One way to show your gratitude for the opportunity to help others is to do just that. Wise leaders are sincerely grateful for the opportunity to help others, and they do so with graciousness.

Paul has found that being helped by some people can be a painful experience because they lack graciousness. It's as if they're saying, "Well, I'll help you, but it's a big inconvenience. I don't know why I'm even bothering, but I'll do it." Some "helpers" convey such a sense of martyrdom and make such a big deal out of their assistance that you wish they hadn't bothered. Such people are not grateful for the opportunity to help; they see it as a burden rather than a blessing. Gracious helpers would say, "I'm glad to be helping you, and it's something I truly want to do, not something I'm doing grudgingly."

We believe that helping behavior is a natural inclination; children, for example, seem always to be glad for the opportunity to be helpful. Not everyone needs help, of course, just as not everyone is open to accepting help, even when they need it, so you should be grateful when the opportunity to help someone appears.

It's worth noting that judgment comes into play here. Like children who want to help but don't know what they're doing, grownups may also "help" in a way that doubles the work instead of cutting it in half. In such cases, you might find yourself telling the would-be helper, "Thanks very much, but I'd rather just do it myself." This is likely to hurt the helper. It indicates that you're not valuing the giver's generosity, graciousness, and good intentions. Instead, you're looking only at the result of what they do.

Thus a part of gratitude may involve suspending judgment. Consider that if a child makes something for you, you are grateful even if their gift is a blotchy mess. You might also value those acts of kindness offered by other adults, regardless of the quality of the help they provide. Our society places a large premium on outcome and tends to disregard intention. Leaders should seek a balance between outcome and intention, showing that both are appreciated.

When you offer to help someone—whether by offering a kind word, being a good listener when they need someone to talk to, lending your hand to physical tasks, or providing expertise—you feel good when your offer is accepted. When your assistance is rejected, though, you're left to wonder: Did they think I didn't have anything to offer, or did they think that my help came with strings attached and would obligate them in some way? Why was my offer not accepted? Did I misperceive that help was needed? Maybe the person you offered to help needed to be self-sufficient. If someone asks for your help, you might ask first how you can be most helpful. People often don't ask for help or accept its offer, so you may experience a natural feeling of gratefulness for the opportunity to share some aspect of yourself when your offer is accepted.

Wise Leaders Are Grateful for Their Gifts and Talents

You can show that you're grateful for your gifts and talents by *using* them. The notion of "use it or lose it" lives in the biblical parable about coins, which once were called "talents." If a man buried his talents instead of putting them to some good use, God was not pleased. Make use of what you've been given and try to expand and strengthen what you have. You do so through your actions as well as your words.

Gratitude for your gifts, in part, is about giving thanks. Genuine words of gratitude have power, but when you take your words a step further and align your "walk" with your "talk," the power of your words increases. Be mindful of what your gifts are and accept responsibility for developing them. Gifts are rarely given in full-blown form; they must be cultivated and developed. Developing, using, and sharing your gifts constitutes both an opportunity and an obligation. You have an obligation to bring your gifts forward—not to waste or hoard them—for your own benefit and the benefit of the world.

Too often, people have been given wonderful gifts but choose not to use them. One person may have a beautiful voice but refuses to sing in public; another may be a good cook but won't prepare food for others. Imagine if Paul, a gifted speaker, said, "I have this gift of being able to speak to groups, small and large, but I choose not to speak anymore. I don't want to bother." Choosing not to use your gifts shows a lack of respect for the gift itself and for the giver. Whether you see your gifts as coming from your genetic heritage, from the universe, from life, or from God, you have an obligation to develop and share them. The Bible admonishes, "To whom much is given, much is required." Those words remind you that your gifts are to be shared, not hoarded, and that the more you have been given, the more you have the responsibility to share.

Everyone has gifts. People tend to define their gifts narrowly, for example, "I'm really smart" or "I'm a great athlete" or "I'm great at singing." Some of the most powerful people we know are some of the simplest people, but they've been given the gifts of love, generosity, and kindness, and they express those gifts with all their heart. They may not be super-smart or accomplished in other ways, but they are impressive nonetheless. If you examine the critical people in any organization, people like these often come to mind.

Paul has such a person in his organization: Calvin, who runs the mailroom. If Calvin were not there, the organization would be markedly different, and not just because he does an efficient job of handling the mail. Paul might find another capable mailroom person, but he would have a hard time finding someone else with the generosity of spirit that Calvin brings to his work. He constantly radiates a feeling of caring toward others. Calvin shares that incredible gift every day with everyone in the organization. When people like Calvin die, the gift of their heart has made an impact that is felt deeply and long remembered.

Recently Paul received one of those little quizzes in the mail that make you stop and think. It said: "Name the last five Pulitzer Prize winners, name the last five Heisman Trophy winners, and name the last five Nobel Prize winners." Of course, most people cannot come close to doing that. Then came the next questions: "Name three teachers who made a difference in your life. Name five people who have loved you unconditionally and who made you feel special." We can all do that!

So then the question becomes: What's really important? Is it the accomplishment? Is it the talent expressed in the act of writing or running with a football, or is it the talent expressed in making a difference in other people's lives, in making their world richer, and in making their sense of humanity more complete? Well, the answer is pretty clear, so talents are much broader than the way people often tend to view them.

About Being Grateful

At one level, gratefulness is a feeling, and from that feeling springs a desire to express it. Gratefulness can be expressed in words, images, or symbols, internally or externally. You can choose to keep it to yourself or share it with other people or with the universe. It can be expressed aloud or silently. You can demonstrate a level of appreciation or a feeling of gratefulness by presenting someone with a tangible gift.

Our belief is that gratitude goes beyond these varied expressions of gratefulness, however; it's also an attitude—a mind-set. If you have an entitlement mentality rather than an attitude of gratitude, it is far less likely that you will experience feelings of gratefulness.

Gratitude emanates from the heart. When Paul has a feeling of gratitude, it starts somewhere in the middle of his chest, not in his head. When someone touches him through an act of kindness or does something that is meaningful to him, the meaning is made in his heart, not in his mind. Gratitude is one of the few things whose meaning is created at the emotional level much more than at the mental level. Gratitude is this welling-up of a feeling in your heart, a sense of warmth and overflowing that occurs somewhere in your chest.

When that happens, gratitude is an expression of love—love writ large. If you take love in its largest context, when someone behaves in a loving way toward you, in a way that shows he cares, that he has a loving feeling toward you, or in a way that really helps you, his action tends to engender a feeling of gratitude. In this context, when you receive love and your heart is open to what you are receiving, a feeling of gratitude is naturally evoked.

Consider for a moment the meaning of the word "gratitude." We use some words so often that their deeper meaning can be lost.

Thinking about what it means to be grateful helps to open your heart to the feeling of gratefulness. So if gratitude is related to love—and we believe that it is—ultimately every caring action is an expression of love in some profound way. When we use the word "love" here, we're looking at love from a broad perspective. Like countless others, we have developed a very expansive view of the love in our world.

Wise Leaders Experience Boundless Gratitude

The word "boundless" implies no boundaries whatsoever. Wise leaders tend to be boundless in many respects, and gratitude is only one of them. Wise leaders tend not to put boundaries around things but rather to remove boundaries. When we discuss gratitude, we're suggesting the kind of gratitude that can be endless and limitless, like an artesian well of possibility that keeps pouring forth. Place boundaries or limits on such a force and you risk capping that well and limiting what comes out, perhaps eventually shutting it down entirely. Similarly, place limits on expressions of gratitude and you risk limiting the potential for what might occur among the people in your organization. Starting with a sense of boundless gratitude is a way of letting that well of possibility spring forth in all its healing, invigorating power.

Gratitude is a well that never runs dry. Give it away, as we observed earlier, and you still have just as much as you had when you started. Love and trust are like that too. In fact, most of the principles of wise leadership work in that same way. Because the ultimate source of wise leadership is divine wisdom, it follows that the principles of wise leadership are boundless. In part, wise leadership is about laying claim to those very principles that have the power to enrich and broaden your existence; they are not limiting or limited in any way. Boundless gratitude is only one of them.

The Importance of Being Grateful for Divine Guidance

We believe that divine guidance is present regardless of your belief system. What varies is your awareness and acceptance of divine guidance, your sensitivity to it. Nonetheless, we are convinced from our personal experience that divine guidance exists, operating in mysterious ways in everyone's lives. Clearly, some people do not subscribe to this viewpoint, and we respect their belief (or lack of belief). However, there is an advantage to assuming that divine guidance does exist and to being grateful for it. In the same way that gratitude begets gratitude and strikes a responsive chord in others, a similar principle operates in relation to the divine: the belief and acceptance of divine guidance, coupled with gratitude for that assistance, increases the role of divine guidance in your life. In other words, gratitude for divine guidance begets more divine guidance.

Being grateful for divine guidance implies that you believe in it and accept it. As a result, you tap into a boundless source of possibility, a power source that would be frightening if it weren't so wonderful. You can't help but be grateful. If you truly have the sense that divine guidance is at work in your life, your sense of optimism, inner peace, and acceptance will also grow. An entire array of gifts is available to you every moment with the single act of accepting divine guidance. You get the full package, a major "Blue Light Special."

We also believe that acceptance and gratitude for divine guidance determine how difficult or benign it will be, but the guidance is always there for all of us. If you choose not to accept it, divine guidance will still be operating, but the lessons facing you will be a much tougher. If you accept the lessons and are grateful for their presence in your life, then you move on to the next lesson. If not, you enter into a kind of "tough love" situation; it's necessary for you to master each lesson before you can move on to the next one. Keep resisting and you'll have to stay after class longer, writing on the board X number of times, "I will not ignore this lesson."

On the other hand, having a sense of gratitude and embracing divine guidance allow you to move much more smoothly through life to the next situation. The added bonus is that divine guidance gives you a sense of never being alone, of having the most powerful partner anyone could have, as well as an endless resource for wisdom.

To become The Wise Leader:

- Have an attitude of gratitude.
- Be mindful of life's blessings.
- Be grateful for the help and support you receive.
- Be grateful for progress.
- Be grateful for obstacles and adversaries, for they may be your best teachers.
- Be grateful for love received.
- Be grateful for love accepted.
- Be grateful for the opportunity to help others.
- Be grateful for your gifts and talents.
- Experience boundless gratitude.
- Be grateful for divine guidance.

CHAPTER 13

The Wisdom of Keeping a Focus on the Now

All of us have a mind, a body, and a spirit. Each of these is functioning in our *now*, our present moment. When these three aspects are integrated and balanced we are able to be at our best. By increasing our understanding and our awareness of these aspects of ourselves we can increase our effectiveness as human beings and as leaders.

Wise leaders have the ability to see the present moment clearly. They understand the power of the present moment, and they are able to focus their full attention on it. Whether they're focusing on people, events, or ideas, wise leaders focus on the *now* in a way that allows them to capitalize on the potential embedded in the present moment. When a leader engages others, listens to others, and focuses on others in a way that shows the leader is fully present in the moment, the power of the present moment expands. He or she uses the moment to solve problems and increase understanding. But the wise leader is also alert to the opportunities inherent in the present that allow the creation of a desired future.

Wise leaders understand that the present *now* is the building block to the future *now*. By taking full advantage of the *now* in their thinking, acting, and being—moment by moment—wise leaders have the power to shape the future.

Focusing on the Now

When you think about it, the *now* is all we really have. The gift that each of us is given is to live each day as it comes. The actions we take are in the present. We can't act on yesterday or tomorrow. Yesterday is gone; tomorrow isn't here yet. It's all about today. We can think about the future and try to plan for it, and we can act today in ways that might affect the future, but we're still acting in the *now*. So we must be more aware of the present and spend less time thinking of the past or the future.

It's difficult for any of us to focus on what is truly important. Our lives are a jumble of events and influences. Just getting through the day can feel like a major accomplishment. And we compound that difficulty by worrying and fretting far too much about what was or what might be. All this noise detracts from our ability to focus on what we can actually affect: the present. Being wise is being attuned to the moment. A focus on this moment allows you to sift through the noise and confusion surrounding you.

Make no mistake, however: keeping our attention focused on the *now* is not easy. It's like trying to steer a boat on the ocean. One minute you're on course but the next minute, thrown off by wind or current, you're off course. Constant adjustments are necessary to stay on course. Those adjustments of attention occur in the present moment. Being present in the moment is a constant challenge, not an achievement that can be savored.

Truly listening to others also requires being present in the moment. If you are actually thinking about something a person did wrong, or about something you intend to tell him, you're not paying attention. You can only attend in the moment. The same is true for trying to focus on a problem. Each second that goes by brings in new data, new thoughts, new challenges. So how do we keep our focus on the *now* without becoming overwhelmed and exhausted?

The key is to learn to put something down before picking up the next thing. Those of us who have a tendency to take on more and more will find that we're straying further and further from the *now*. If you pick up too much stuff, you start to drop and break the things you've been holding and you lose track of what you have. Staying in the *now* is learning to set something down before you pick up something else. In this era of "multitasking," such a notion may sound quaint. But the truth is that there's another word for multitasking: distracted. Wise leaders must plan for the future, of course, because one of their roles is to *create* the future. But if they get so lost in planning for the future that they lose their current focus, trouble is always the result.

Though it can be difficult to stay in the moment, we get cues and clues when we are straying from it. When we become aware that we're drifting, we have a choice. We can wake up and try to refocus on what we're doing, or take our loss of attention as a clue that maybe we're currently focusing on the wrong thing. Life isn't just something that happens to us. (Some folks are fond of saying that life is what happens when you're making other plans.) We have the power to redirect our life and move it in a better direction. Maybe we just need to relax, or stretch, or get up and walk around a bit. Whenever your ability to stay focused is waning—whatever the reason may be—you have the power to choose another *now*. There are times when external forces will control the events taking place around us. Even then, we always have a choice of how we respond to those events.

Being Fully Present in the Present

Being fully present can be deceptively difficult. In fact, many of us must learn this practice the hard way. As Paul's mother lay dying, he spent countless hours in the hospital room with her. The shades were drawn so he had no awareness of what was happening outside—no sense of time passing, or of the weather, or even if it was day or night. With the television turned off so she could rest, there was no external stimulation. All Paul had was a keen awareness that each moment he spent with his mother meant one less moment that he would be able to spend with her. Paul had a powerful sense of being there in that quiet room solely for her and living in the same moment that she was. If you knew Paul you would know that was not his usual way of living his life. His job at that time kept him on the road four or five days a week, and when he was home he had to try to oversee a complex national-level organization. People who knew him found his life frenetic and disjointed. To go from flitting and flying about to sitting silently in a hospital room was a jarring exercise in deceleration. During that painful period Paul began to appreciate the power of the moment.

Being in the moment in that room combined a sense of hyperawareness with a concurrent feeling of blending into a *now* that blurred the barriers of time and space. On the one hand Paul became very aware of that hospital room; he learned its every detail. He knew each visitor and what was said. He knew the sounds and smells of the hospital. But there was also a sense of just *being*—of blending in with it all: this is where I am, this is my present. He came to see that there was no reason to worry about what was happening back at his office, or what events he was missing, because they were out of his reach; he had different priorities. So there, in that room, he just *was*. The *now* was all he had and all that mattered.

Paul could have withdrawn into himself and focused on his grief. But he made the choice to be as fully present as possible. He chose not to retreat or to redirect his thoughts to something else. An avid reader, he had several books with him. Under normal circumstances, given the gift of uninterrupted time, he would have immersed himself in a book. But he chose not to read. He chose just to be there with his mother even though there were long stretches of time when she was asleep and not present for him. His final gift to her was to be available. Being in the *now* is staying available to those around us. It is a great gift to them.

Staying available to others is one of the hardest things we can do. Our minds are wonderful machines that keep on ticking. They keep working even while we sleep! Thousands of thoughts swirl through them; the more responsibility we have, it seems, the more there is to engage our busy brains. Steve admits that when he talks with others, there are times when his mind wanders to other topics. When he catches himself, he apologizes briefly and asks the person to repeat what was just said. He has found that very often people are not offended; in fact, they're pleased that he really wants to hear what they have to say. Steve is far from alone in the mind-wandering department. We all do it. His authenticity of admitting it, though, creates a bond with the person with whom he was talking.

Now Is Where We Are

Humans share the gift of not having to be physically present to be somewhere. Our fertile and creative minds allow us to be thinking of China while sitting in Chicago. The ability to think creatively can take us wherever we wish to go in seconds.

That gift is also our curse, however, because it is hard to be fully present when it's so easy to be somewhere else instead. Our imaginations even allow us to be somewhere we have never been before because we can go wherever we can imagine. Modern technology also allows us to be physically one place but mentally somewhere else. That can certainly lead to a distracted life. Our memories further complicate matters by allowing us to be somewhere in time that is not the current time. We can relive our first date in high school or last summer's vacation. With all those competing thoughts in our brains it's little wonder that we have difficulty staying in the moment.

But the multidimensional *now* requires us to be in the present mentally, physically, and spiritually. We have to be focused mentally on what is happening, and we have to be attuned to our physical environment so we can focus on what is important in our present. Steve uses meditation and conscious breathing to help him become centered in the *now*. He chooses a place where he can see a natural setting, which helps him to relax into a peaceful, meditative state. As he does so, the surrounding environment becomes less important.

Recently Paul visited a coffee shop where J. K. Rowling wrote parts of her famous Harry Potter books. This rowdy, loud, crowded space was the opposite of what Steve seeks for his meditations. And yet somehow Rowling found inspiration in that thoroughly distracting environment. Perhaps she was motivated by the view out the window of the gray stone parapets of Edinburgh or by the cemetery just below the window, where she found on the headstones several of the names she used in her best-selling books.

On another occasion, walking down a busy street in Chicago, Paul saw a young woman sitting on the sidewalk, meditating. Two hours later Paul passed the same spot and she was still sitting there—peaceful, still, and serene. Wherever she was, Paul thought, it wasn't on that street in Chicago. The point: there is no one best environment for meditation. Each of us must find the one that allows us to be centered and in the moment.

People who meditate describe themselves as being very much in the *now*—so much so that they are undistracted by their surroundings. Naturally, a busy leader will find it difficult to achieve such a state in the midst of a hectic workday, but a bit of that sense will go a long way to help refocus us on the *now*.

A wise leader can also use mental imagery as a means of staying focused. Paul knows a special spot in Utah that gives him great peace. A mountain stream runs through a spectacular canyon and trees line the stream as it gurgles its way down the canyon. This is where Paul goes to refocus, to find a center and be quiet in his head. And when he's not in that peaceful setting Paul still calls up that image in his head—when he has to visit the dentist, for example. Ironically, this kind of mental imagery is the furthest thing from being in the *now*, and yet it provides Paul a helpful alternative *now* that keeps him centered.

The *now* that most leaders face is full of distraction and confusion; so many factors conspire to knock leaders off center. In addition, there is the constant internal distraction of thinking how we ought to be, need to be, or should be. What's necessary is to accept *where* we are and *how* we are at any point. It's not about where we ought to be; it's about where we *are*. There is a continual interplay between the outer world and its demands and the inner world and its demands. The body has its own needs; when its needs arise, the mind and spirit take a back seat. But the mind has needs too. Sometimes we need order and logic; sometimes we need fun and frivolity. And the spirit has its own needs. We need a sense of peace and purpose. All of these conflicting and complementary needs are in constant interplay with each other.

Of those three elements that make up our humanity, it is the spirit that most demands the *now*. The mind and body can be fooled into thinking one is someplace else or in some other time. The spirit *knows* that only the present moment is available to us, and that's what is most important. The spirit cries out for the moment. If you're feeling pain it is only the pain of the moment that's important—not the pain you felt last week or the pain you might feel tomorrow. If you're elated, it is only the elation of that moment that counts.

When Paul prays, he seeks the peacefulness of the moment, not the peacefulness that might come as a result of his prayer. The act of prayer itself creates a feeling of peace. When Steve meditates, he meditates in the moment that is happening right *now*, not in the meditation he might do next week. The spirit lives in the *now* naturally, and that can bring the other parts that are more subject to distraction into alignment.

Focus Our Thinking in the Now

The brain can really get in the way of our focusing on the *now*. In fact, you might say that the brain has a mind of its own. It tends to jump between the past and the future. Getting it to focus on the present can be challenging. Staying in the *now* means staying aware. One of Paul's techniques for staying in the moment is stepping outside himself; this allows him to be both a participant and an observer. A high need for control will impede this ability. It's necessary to relinquish some control momentarily in order to observe what is happening and see where the flow is going. If you try to control the moment, you're actually trying to force the flow of the moment in the direction you desire it to go, rather than allowing it to unfold in new and sometimes pleasantly surprising ways. As you become an observer of yourself, you stop thinking about tomorrow or yesterday and simply stay in the moment. If you're emotionally attached to what is happening you lose your sense of detachment and your ability to observe.

As Paul was grieving for his mother, a part of him was grieving and another part was observing his grief and giving him permission to feel his grief. Years before, when Paul's father passed, he had failed to give himself permission to feel his grief. His inability to allow the grieving process to unfold naturally made his grieving less authentic—and thus less healing. Only in stepping back from your emotions and being an observer can you really find your authenticity; in doing so you give yourself permission to feel (or to be however you are) at that moment. By allowing yourself to step back from yourself you are both there and not there simultaneously.

Some events outside of us focus our attention on the moment. Danger is one. Pleasure is another. Being screamed at or threatened tends to focus your attention, just as the act of making love focuses your attention. Most of the time, though, we can choose what to focus on and how to be. If a bear is chasing you, focus. If you're sitting in your office chatting with a staff member, you might not have the same need to focus.

Steve employs a routine that creates self-discipline when he feels the need to focus. If he has a job to do that requires focused thinking, he turns off the phone. He might go to a more private space and close the door. Sometimes people mistake focus for not doing anything, mistakenly equating thinking with idleness. In fact, some of the hardest work a wise leader does takes place inside his or her head. Outside there may be no visible signs that anything is going on, but inwardly the leader can be teeming with ideas and solutions.

A friend of Steve's was planning to remodel his kitchen. The architect sent him the plans along with a bill for ten hours of work. The friend called the architect to complain. He said the plans could not have taken more than one hour to draw up. The architect agreed but said that it took him nine hours of thinking to come up with his drawings. Steve's friend replied, "Okay, I like the plan, but please don't spend any more time thinking about it. I can't afford it." We tend to believe that thought is free and that doing is what takes real effort and earns the money. But doing without thinking won't get you far.

Similarly, we tend to see self-discipline as external and physical. We use self-discipline, for instance, to exercise or diet or even spend our time in an organized way. The self-discipline required to stay in the *now* is a much deeper and more internal kind of discipline. This kind of self-discipline is not about staying on a diet—it's about having a sense of self that allows you to value who you are rather than to abuse who you are by failing to take care of yourself.

The same is also true for the self-discipline required to run an organization. Staying focused on the *now* is a form of self-discipline that values the purpose and deepest core of the organization and the people in it. This kind of self-discipline resides at the very deepest part of our spirit; it is the core of doing the right things for the right reasons. The self-discipline required to stay focused on the moment is not some sort of power trip by the leader. Rather, it is an affirmative set of personal choices that put you more closely in touch with the moment and the *now* and the things you ought to be thinking about and focusing on.

Focus Our Doing in the Now

It's important to remember that all we can actually *do* is here, in the *now*. We can't redo last week or do next week. We can only do what is present. Not long after Paul's mother passed away, as he was leaving a parking lot he found himself waiting at the tollbooth. Finally the attendant, who had been watching him patiently, asked, "Are you planning to pay?" Paul realized that he was *doing* the *now* but not being *in* the *now*. Though he was physically in his car at the tollbooth, he certainly wasn't focused on that moment. His mind was somewhere else.

In a lovely little book called *Mindfulness,* Ellen Langer brings to our attention how little mindfulness exists in today's world. Have you ever bumped into a mannequin at a department store and excused yourself? That's mindlessness—that is, being out of focus on the *now*. Until something is invented that allows us to subdivide our physical selves, we can exist physically in only one place at one time. It's good if our minds and spirits are there with us too.

One way of staying focused on what we're doing in the *now* is to connect it to the future. If we're exercising, we are doing it in the *now*, but that exercise also affects our future selves. Similarly, if we smoke cigarettes, we are also affecting our future selves. Focusing on what we are doing in the present is, in part, making a values choice. We are choosing how we spend our time and also placing a value on our choice. Choosing to exercise or choosing to smoke are about self-discipline, to be sure, but they are also choices that show how we value ourselves. An example: Paul loves sweets. He *knows* the nonnutritional calories in sweets aren't good for him, but when he chooses to eat a piece of candy, he has chosen to reward his present self at the expense of his future self. He has talked himself into thinking that he deserves that piece of candy, or needs it to be happy. But he has made a values choice to choose the *now* over the future.

What we do in the *now* is critical. We are deciding our lives in the future; if we are leaders, we are deciding the lives of others by how we choose to focus on the *now*. All of us seek gratification in various ways; self-discipline is a choice between instant gratification and delayed gratification. And the most powerful manner in which we can exercise self-discipline is to discipline ourselves to stay focused in the *now*—to be aware and present so that what we do reflects mindfulness.

Focus Our Being in the Now

We pointed out earlier that our spirits, our beings, are always in the *now*. They can be nowhere else. Religious teachings tell us that our spirits are eternal, but they are also quite temporal. Why? Because our beings know that they cannot be anywhere other than where they are at the present moment. The spirit demands to be fed in the present. It cannot be fooled into thinking it is somewhere else or sometime else. We can fool our minds and our bodies, but we can never fool the essence of what is truly us.

Steve and Paul have spent a great many hours talking about getting in touch with their higher selves because they know that their higher selves are the source of their ability to think and feel and communicate and be at peace. And yet it's striking how little time we tend to spend on actually making that connection. We take it for granted. When we connect with our spirits, which can only happen by being in the *now*, then we become able to tap into what they have to offer. While our spirits demand to be fed, they are constantly feeding us. And by the way, we don't need to feed our spirits because they *need* feeding—we need to feed them because we grow by feeding them.

The duality of our relationship with our spirits is a reciprocal relationship—the Golden Rule writ large. We care for our bodies and our bodies care for us. We care for our minds and our minds care for us. We care for our spirits and our spirits care for us. We care for others and they care for us. We are at our most powerful when we are feeding our spirits—not because they need us to do so but because *we* are at our best when we do so. When we operate out of this mode of mutual caring, we are happiest and most at peace with our world.

Of course, if we become cut off from our spirits, our connection to them can wither away. Our spirits need this connection, and they need us to *want* to be connected. When our thoughts, words, and actions are not in accord with our spirits' true nature, it withers. When our spirits are thriving, we are happy, fulfilled, and energized. When our spirits wither, we are miserable, unfulfilled, and more susceptible to illness and disease. (The word "disease" is really about being ill at ease—"dis-ease," which is the ultimate reaction to an unnurtured spirit.) But many factors can empower the spirit—for example, when we are able to manifest our gifts, or master our life lessons, or make the world a better place.

Focus on the Foreground and the Background of Our Now

What we refer to as the "foreground" of our *now* is pretty obvious. When we focus on the foreground we're paying attention to what is here in front of our noses, to our immediate circumstances. The foreground cries out for our attention. Those aspects of what we refer to as the foreground are noisy, colorful, beautiful, distracting, or even unpleasant. They are often what we choose to focus on because they're right in front of us.

But it's hard to consider the foreground without also noticing the background. Steve has a beautiful painting in his living room that commands attention. That's foreground. Focus your attention elsewhere, however—say, on a fascinating conversation—and that same painting recedes to an insignificant place in your consciousness. Foreground is all about what we focus our attention on.

Often some aspects of our foreground are hard to ignore. The phone rings, and continues ringing, and we must decide whether to answer it or let it ring. Obviously that's foreground. Knowing that we need to return a phone call ourselves can be background. The desire to make that phone call is somewhere in our consciousness, but it isn't front and center. When Paul was a superintendent he used to answer the phone because he thought it might be important. Most of the time he found it was a telemarketer calling instead. That lesson caused him to start moving ringing phones to the background of his consciousness.

The present moment—the *now*—always has a foreground and a background. Guided by their values and priorities, leaders can focus attention in a way that highlights aspects in the foreground of the *now*, or aspects in the background of the *now*, or both. Wise leaders are skilled at shifting issues and events from background to foreground and vice versa. By setting the context and framing the aspects of the *now*, wise leaders can increase or decrease the energy flowing into the foreground or background of the present moment.

Leaders often spend so much of their time on foreground activities that they forget that the context provided by background must also be considered. This brings to mind those companies that focus on quarterly growth but, in doing so, neglect long-term profits and growth. The constant tug-of-war is between short-term versus long-term, urgent versus important. It's all too easy to allow the urgent to push out the important; wise leaders strive to maintain a balance between the two. Wise leaders use the foreground to frame what is unfolding in the present and then fit that into the larger, longer-range context. Wise leaders know that a movie is more than a stack of photographs. The photos capture the moments; the movie tells the story.

Using the concept of "framing" is another way to look at this duality. Framing determines what is important and what is not—frames draw attention to the picture. Think of having a big picture and placing a smaller frame on it. Moving the frame highlights different pictures within the big picture. There are many different images, yet remove the frame and you're left with the same image that was there before. Wise leaders understand the difference between background and foreground as they frame their pictures of their organization. Artists (and wise leaders) have a sensitive eye that understands what parts of the picture should stand out from the background, and they know how to draw the eye toward what is important. Unskilled framers (and less wise leaders) just slap a frame around a picture without worrying about what is important.

It's easy to confuse the foreground with the background. It's like missing the forest for the trees. Focus on the tree instead of the forest and you miss the bigger picture. And if you look only at the bark, you can even miss the tree! You have to use judgment to determine what is important. It can be difficult to help people see the bigger picture, particularly if they spend all their time dealing with minutiae. As the old saying goes, if the only tool you have is a hammer, everything looks like a nail. Helping people see that they may need a different tool is an important part of the wise leader's role.

Now Is the Building Block for the Next Now

Tomorrow is always built on today. But when tomorrow arrives, tomorrow is today. Tomorrow has become our new *now*. And from the vantage point of tomorrow, today has become yesterday. Each moment is clearly a building block for the next.

A common mistake we make is to consider change from too large a perspective. If you think of change as an angle, a tiny adjustment at the vortex changes the angle dramatically as it goes outward. Change requires us to see where we wish to end up, but we can make the decision to approach a large change by effecting a series of very small changes in the *now*. Operating on a more modest set of changes in the short term can pave the way for huge changes over time. One reason that some leaders fail is that they try to change too much, too fast. We may desire big changes next year, but right *now* all we have is the next twenty minutes. How can we use the *now* to affect our next *now*?

A key skill for a wise leader is the ability to be a reflective thinker; with reflection comes perspective—the interplay of foreground and background—which brings the bigger picture into clearer focus. Gaining perspective makes it clear how small decisions in the present can have a huge impact for good in the future.

Consider the question, "How do you eat an elephant?" A bite at a time, of course. By eating a bite each day, eventually you'll be able to consume the whole pachyderm. First, however, be clear about what you want to get done. That comes through reflection: you want to eat the elephant. Forget that and you might end up eating cauliflower, a piece of bark, or parts of a cow. Keep your eye on the prize while taking the little steps that will get you to your goal. The background is the future: eating the elephant. The foreground is *now*: taking one bite, and then the next bite. The wise leader understands the difference between incrementalism that makes no difference and incrementalism that can lead to big things. Staying focused on the goal even while you also focus on the *now* is the path to success.

Wise leaders also understand exactly which part of their elephant they want to eat next. They don't lunge at the enormous meal like a hungry lion; they have a plan. Wise leaders have perspective and an orientation that goes beyond self-discipline, which assure them that if they keep building one block at a time, or taking one step at a time (or one bite at a time), the cumulative effect is geometric, not linear. Think of it as building a pyramid—laying each stone carefully at the base and then at each succeeding level until the capstone is set in place and a structure has been built that will stand the test of time.

Wise leaders also know that eating elephants or building pyramids are not always easy or pleasant processes. You might rather be eating a chocolate bar or watching television. There's immediate gratification in the candy and the TV, but if your goal is to eat an elephant (or build a great organization), you can eat all the chocolate bars you want, but you won't be any closer to the goal. Often our long-term goals entail a good many unpleasant days spent in doing little, sometimes not-so-pleasant tasks. Long-term benefit can require short-term sacrifice.

Shaping the Future through the Now of Our Present

The wise leader knows that the quality of our future is shaped by the quality of our present—that is, by the quality that we choose to make of our present. If we want a different result in our future, we must change what we are doing today. Thinking again of that poor elephant metaphor, it may be not enough simply to want to *eat* the elephant—you might want to cook it first. That would certainly change the quality of the dining experience. Likewise, it's not enough just to live your life; it helps greatly to decide the kind of life you want to live. And it's not enough merely to have a successful organization if it's not a place where you or anyone else wants to work.

Everything we do *now* shapes and affects our future. Knowing that, we must ask ourselves what we want to do in the present that will contribute to the future. How do we want to see the future evolve? This requires that we stay conscious and aware of what we are doing. And it's about choice—that is, choosing what kind of future we wish to create. Wise leaders are in touch with their consciousness, but they are also in touch with their conscience. This awareness allows them to make the right choices for the right reasons.

The right choices, made for the right reasons, will create long-term dividends. As the future moves closer to the present we become more aware of how our choices and the wisdom (or lack of wisdom) of our choices has created a certain quality to our lives. A wise leader understands that wise choices benefit others. When choices are made that benefit others and a broader world, our *now* has created the kind of future that we all desire to live in.

To become The Wise Leader:

- Focus on the *now*.
- Be fully present in the present moment.
- Know that *now* is where you are.
- Be able to focus your thinking in the *now*.
- Be able to focus your doing in the *now*.
- Be able to focus your being in the *now*.
- Be able to focus on the background of *now*.
- Be able to focus on the foreground of *now*.
- Know that *now* is always the building block for the next *now*.
- Know how to shape the future through the present *now*.

Part IV

CHAPTER 14

The Wisdom of Serving Others

Everyone, deep down, wants life to have meaning—and we especially want our own lives and the lives of those we love to have meaning. Both of us certainly hold that belief, and we believe the key to a meaningful life is our service to others. Why? Because service is tied inextricably to our life's purpose.

Think of it this way: all of life is interconnected. When we serve others we serve life itself; in so doing we serve a higher power. Because we are part of the fabric of life, when we serve others we also serve ourselves. We all want to be happy and to feel fulfilled in all aspects of our lives. One certain way to achieve happiness and fulfillment is through serving and helping others. It's almost impossible to help others and not feel good about it. Wise leaders choose to serve others not only because of the way such service makes them feel, but also because they see service to others as a way of truly serving the divine.

Not all forms of service are equal. Some are more powerful and more meaningful than others. Serving the needy, the weak, the infirm, the less fortunate, the disabled, the disadvantaged, and the impoverished are powerful forms of service. One of the highest forms of service, though, is service to children, for children are a sacred trust; children embody our future. Our service to others leaves an imprint, a legacy. When that legacy enhances and furthers life, a form of energy alchemy occurs and a physical legacy is transformed into a spiritual legacy.

Serving Others Serves Our Divine Purpose

Serving others is a core value in most spiritual traditions. When we look at our own life purposes, somewhere among them is a component that deals with serving other people. Every mission that is worthwhile in some way incorporates the need to serve others. We believe that at a spiritual level we're all connected and part of a unified whole.

Steve remembers when his younger son married and his older son served as best man. The wedding took place on Father's Day. Steve's older son had forgotten to bring his Father's Day present. During that weekend, however, he gave a heartwarming toast, threw a bachelor party, and gave a very generous gift that helped his brother afford a honeymoon that would otherwise have been out of reach. Steve told him, "The way you treated your brother is the best Father's Day gift I could have received. I don't need anything more than just seeing the way you treated your brother." As a father, Steve could have had no greater sense of pride or joy than watching one brother serving the other. What might it look like at the macro level if every one of us served all others as our brothers and sisters? What greater way to bring joy and happiness to the Father of us all?

Serving Others Is the Key to Personal Happiness and Fulfillment

The happiest people we know are those involved in serving other people, or who at least have an orientation of service toward others. The correlation may not be perfect, but it is surely extremely high. We would be challenged to think of someone who has decided on a path of service who has not found a large measure of happiness and fulfillment as a result. It's not just a matter of saying, "Okay, I'm here to serve." Rather, it's the process of serving others well and actually helping other people that makes us feel good. Helping other people engenders a feeling of appreciation within the person who has been helped. When that appreciation is expressed—even in a subtle way, such as body language—the helper feels happy. When you know you have done something good for another person and they have benefited from your action, you feel great.

Sooner or later, many people who have made a lot of money end up trying to find a way to serve others in some way. They start foundations, or they decide to quit their work and do something in service of others. They volunteer. Paul was involved with America's Promise and with the Board of Communities and Schools. When he talked to board members who had a great deal of wealth, every one of them agreed that one of the best things they had done in their lives was to mentor a child or to tutor someone who needed their help. They didn't want to talk about their wealth or their appearances on TV or on magazine covers. They talked about how great they felt when they saw a child learning or when they did something for a child. The interest paid on serving others is exponentially greater than the interest rate paid by your bank.

We believe that students should be required to take part in service activities in school. How else will they learn it? If young people have never experienced the opportunity of serving other people, most of them are going to say, "I don't want to do that. I'm busy. I've got other things to do. I've got my own life." Yet when they experience performing service for others, *they get it.*

Years ago Paul was involved in a program in which kids were made to do service for twelve weeks. They were unhappy about it, very unhappy. They even came to the superintendent's office and protested. They thought the service activities were a distraction from their academics. Paul replied simply, "Well, it's part of the curriculum, we got a grant to do this, and we have to fulfill the grant."

What happened next was quite interesting. After the twelve-week program, the students returned to their regular courses. They were no longer required to carry out their service project. When the school district did a follow-up study, however, they found that 95 percent of the students involved continued to do their service activity even when it was no longer required. Asked why, the students said, "Well, I didn't want to do it at first, but it was really great. I loved going to that nursing home and the people were so interesting. I loved talking to them, and a little bit of my time meant so much to them."

These young people had learned the leveraging value of service and how powerful it can be. Instead of a leveraged buyout, you get a leveraged "buy-in"—a little bit goes a very long way. What's more, there is a ripple effect. You start a chain reaction when you do something good for somebody else. The effects do not stop with that person but spread outward.

Service is the key that unlocks the door of happiness. Picture a wise man talking to a young boy seeking wisdom.

The boy asks, "What is the secret of happiness?"

And the wise man answers, "The secret of happiness is, 'Serve others.'"

Once people go down that path, there's something about it that hooks them. It is one of the answers to people's search for meaning. Where do you find meaning? Do you find it in making dog biscuits? Do you find it in investing in stocks? Perhaps. But serving others is different. Not only does it engage your mind, but it also engages your heart. Ultimately, you need to feed your heart and your soul. And the food for that is in what you give, not in what you take.

Wise Leaders Choose to Serve Others

When Paul was in Prague he met a school principal who had been out of the principalship for twenty years and then returned to it. When Paul asked if he had left for personal or political reasons, the man replied, "Well, for political reasons; the communists wanted me to teach things that were not true, and they wanted me not to teach things that were true, and so I had to make a moral choice."

On the plane returning home, Paul met two Britons. One was a firefighter in eastern England who had raised $20,000 for the New York Fire Department after the terrorist attack of 9/11. Asked why he did that, he replied, "I had no choice." The point is that when you are a moral leader, as was the Czech principal, you make a choice. But if you're a truly wise leader you have no choice because for you there really is no other choice.

The kind of people we have been describing as wise leaders have a navigation system that tells them when they are serving others. It seems pretty clear to us that if you make things better for other people you're engaged in a form of service—and that's what wise leaders do, instinctively and intuitively. Such choices are so intuitive, so instinctive, so natural for the wise leader that often it doesn't even feel as if he's making a choice. His actions are simply a part of his being. *The real choice is to strive to be a wise leader.* When you make that choice, then everything else flows from that choice almost naturally. At a deep level there is no choice because the need to serve is so clear and compelling.

Examine the wise leader and you'll observe some form of service to others. Or look at a place where service to others is unfolding in a significant way, and you can probably trace those actions back to a wise leader. *Like two sides of a coin, service to others and wise leadership are inextricably connected.*

Two sides of a different coin are the words "selfish" and "selfless." Wise leaders operate from the selfless side of things, which is additive and expansive; selfishness is contracting and diminishing. You pull stuff toward you when you are selfish, but when you are selfless you push stuff away. These are two very different ways of looking at and operating in the world. That said, we want to be clear that if you have a focus on serving others it doesn't mean that you cannot benefit from the processes or outcomes that unfold as a result of your actions. If your intention is to serve others, we don't believe you are barred from doing things to improve your own life as well. It's not an either-or proposition. Furthermore, if all you are doing is providing for others and not taking care of yourself, at some point you're going to run yourself into deficit. So it's appropriate to take care of yourself, thus creating a balance that allows you to continue to provide for and serve others.

Serving Others Leaves a Spiritual Legacy

Have you ever thought about how you want to be remembered? One question Paul asks applicants in job interviews—and it always takes them by surprise—is what they would like on their tombstone. Steve asks another version of the same question. He asks, "Your life has run its course and you're looking at your epitaph—what does it say?"

As a superintendent, Paul always thought that his most important work was what he left behind in the people with whom he worked. Because so often you spend days, and weeks, and months developing programs and putting things into place, and the next guy comes along and undoes all your work. Or the school board changes and suddenly everything is different. But what *isn't* different is what you've left behind in the hearts of people. And that's your spiritual legacy.

One of Steve's mentors was a professor at the University of Wisconsin. She chose not to spend her energy writing and publishing books. She used to tell him, "I write my books in people." Because of their relationship and what he learned from her, Steve has always thought of himself as one of her "books." Who's been writing in your book? Here's an empowering thought: Whose books are *you* writing in? Our acts of service, of caring, and of loving kindness are indelibly written in the hearts of the people whom we touch in a special way. When Steve writes a condolence card he uses the phrase that this person "will be remembered in the hearts and loving memories of those whose lives they touched."

Rarely does anyone think, "I'm going to create a spiritual legacy today." Instead we think, "Ah, this person needs some help and I'm going to try to help out, or open a door, or create a connection, or show them a possibility that they hadn't seen." But in the process of performing acts of kindness, or creating growth opportunities for other people, and all of the other things that wise leaders do, we are continually leaving our spiritual footprints in the sands of time and creating a spiritual legacy without even realizing it.

We Create Our Future by What We Teach Our Children

We tend to say we're teaching kids so that they can be successful in the future. We seem to have less awareness that what we're teaching them, and the way we're teaching them, are actually creating the future that they'll live in and, to some extent, the future that *we'll* live in.

Lately this way of looking at the future has been driven home to us in a negative way. While many of us are trying to create the most positive future we can, we see what's happening in terms of terrorism in the world, and read about the Madrasas in Pakistan and the Pesantrens in Indonesia where what children are learning is biased, narrowly focused, and myopic. Along with their religious instruction, children are learning hate and they're learning blame. They're not learning the kinds of things needed to create a positive future, at least from our perspective; instead they're learning to idealize suicide bombers. This is a vivid example of how the power of schools and the power of what we teach actually create the future that is unfolding. It's up to us to determine what kind of future we want. That future can be wonderful and expansive and uplifting, or it can be as destructive as hell on earth.

Two basic human emotions are at work most of the time: fear and trust. More of one usually means less of the other; as one expands the other contracts. What you fear is what is outside your circle. What you trust is what is inside your circle. So the issue is, how big is your circle? In those schools we mentioned in the previous paragraph there are very small circles, where virtually everything outside the circle is something to be feared, hated, and destroyed. Such schools can be found not only in Pakistan or Afghanistan; they also can be found in the United States, sometimes operating right down the street, sometimes in the name of God. Ironically enough, most often we use the name of God to create a sense of, "We're in the right; if you believe as we do, you'll be trusted. If you don't, you're to be feared, excluded, and, in extreme cases, destroyed."

Wise leadership is about making our circles bigger and expanding the notion of trust. To do that it's necessary to operate in a trusting way. Often it is leaders themselves who are incapable of trust. If you can't trust, what kind of example are you creating? If you're a teacher, or a principal, or a district superintendent, and you operate from a base of fear and distrust, how can you possibly pass anything other than fear and distrust on to the children for whom you are responsible? And what kind of world are you creating when you foster such feelings, as opposed to operating from a sense of trust and love and expansion and forgiveness? Wise leaders know the difference and are mindful of the examples they set.

Serving Children Is a Sacred Trust

When you serve people who are defenseless and not totally formed, those who are absolutely dependent on the good will of others, the level of sacred trust required of you becomes vitally important. In such cases you are not serving children merely to be kind; you must serve them because they will not be able to survive without you. Notice how much longer human beings are dependent creatures compared to other animals. For all our strength as a species—our powerful brains and our opposable thumbs—we must get through a very long period of years when our young are defenseless.

We believe that serving children is a sacred trust because life itself is holy. Those who serve children have been given precious lives to care for and guide at a time when they are most vulnerable, impressionable, and malleable. People who work with children help shape the direction of their lives and have an impact on the way those young lives will unfold. We are dealing with a sacred trust because for a period of time a life has been entrusted to you. What are you going to do with it? Do you do something engaging, uplifting, and empowering? Or do you teach that young person to be withdrawn, fearful, and distrustful? Do you give each child in your care the skills and knowledge needed to succeed and thrive? To some extent, those who work with very young children have almost godlike powers over their charges. What can be more sacred than being entrusted with the care and well-being of a child? What we do, individually and collectively, with that sacred trust to a large extent defines us and shapes our future.

The image that comes to mind is the potter's wheel: taking something unformed and rough and trying to create something useful and beautiful. That certainly does imply a high obligation: starting with a lump of pure potential and helping to shape its future. From the national level to the personal level, with all the institutions in between, wise leadership or the lack thereof reflects how well we fulfill this sacred trust.

Serving Children Is One of the Highest Forms of Service

Since we've devoted our professional lives to serving children, clearly we believe that doing so is one of the highest forms of service. We would include the weak and the sick and the aged because they also cannot serve themselves—and if they're not served, they wither and eventually perish.

Stewardship of others calls for extraordinary amounts of effort and caring. But we're not referring only to professional educators. We're talking about parents, too, and everyone else who plays a role that affects the well-being of children, including our elected officials. We're talking about the businessperson who complains about his or her taxes going to maintain schools. We're talking about the proverbial village it takes to raise a child. As caretakers in that village it's important to realize that we are engaged in a high form of service. Not only does it take a village to raise a child, but it also takes a child to ennoble the village. The child gives the village the opportunity to find meaning.

Our role is to help children make the transition from being dependent and defenseless to being empowered and independent. We actually facilitate a transformational process that links one generation to the next. So people who are trying to create a better future can do so through what we, all of us working together, teach our young. Children are the path to the future; the kind of education we provide largely determines what that future will be, because how and what we teach our young will affect how and what they will teach their young.

Serving Others Serves the Divine

Paul is a Christian. He often thinks of Mother Teresa seeing the face of Christ in the beggars she served. She very literally understood that she was serving the divine when she served other people, because God was in everyone she served. That's something that Paul tries hard to remember. He's not Mother Teresa by any means, but sometimes when he sees someone who's terribly deformed or drunk or sick and not doing well, he tries to transform his view of that person by saying, "That is one of God's children. They are as divine as I am." He then sees them through a different lens than the one he might have been using when he first saw them. He focuses on the fact that they are also one of God's creatures.

Steve is Jewish. In similar situations, what goes through his mind is, "But for the grace of God there go I." A different stroke of luck in terms of an injury, or the onset of a latent mental illness, or being made infirm by a severe stroke, and suddenly we become that other person who at first may offend our sensibilities.

Both of us believe that we serve the divine by serving others. How else would you serve the divine? We're sure there may be other, grander ways, but until such time as we are given miraculous powers, we must do what we can by serving that which the divine has created, both in terms of people and in terms of stewardship of the environment.

If we believe that there is a spark of the divine in others, then when we serve others we are almost automatically serving the divine. At our best, we kindle that spark in others and help it to grow. Wise leaders see their leadership role as a precious gift, one that allows them to serve the divine by serving others.

To become The Wise Leader:

- Choose to serve others.
- See serving others as the key to personal happiness and fulfillment.
- Understand that serving others leaves a spiritual legacy.
- Know that we create our future by what we teach our children.
- Know that serving children is one of the highest forms of service.
- See serving children as a sacred trust.
- Help others expand their circle of inclusiveness.
- Help others expand their level of trust.
- Help others reduce their level of fear.
- Know that serving others serves the divine.

CHAPTER 15

The Wisdom of Operating from a Base of Compassion

Wise leaders are compassionate. They understand that all human beings incur problems, difficulties, and illness—or even tragedy and severe personal loss—at various times in their lives. Wise leaders are especially sensitive to the needs of others during such difficult times, and they make an extra effort to be kind and understanding during others' misfortunes. During good times or bad, however, wise leaders continually try to nurture and uplift those around them. They do this not just by the way they treat people, but also by creating climates and cultures that bring out the best in people. They institute programs and organizational structures that help people succeed, thrive, and grow.

All organizations need rules and standards of conduct, of course, but wise leaders know that human behavior is too complex to be bound by a rigid set of unyielding rules. Wise leaders use their authority to bend some rules when it's the right thing to do, and when it's in the best interest of those they lead. They know when it's appropriate to bend the rules to meet the needs of people rather than force people to bend to the rules.

Because of their compassion, wise leaders engender loyalty and appreciation in those around them. They touch our hearts as well as our minds in times of need; consequently, their acts are long remembered. They serve as role models of what we can be like when we are at our best—when we put the Golden Rule into action and truly live and lead by it.

What It Means to Operate from a Base of Compassion

Compassion is something that comes from within. It is archetypal, which is to say that we humans have an innate capacity for it. Once that capacity is activated by our own life experiences, certain external events and circumstances trigger compassionate feelings almost instinctively and automatically. Wise leaders not only have those feelings, but they know how and when to act on them.

True compassion flows from a connection at the heart level. You can think compassionately *about* someone or think empathetically *toward* someone and communicate those feelings, but those actions are quite different from communicating at the heart level. The notion that true compassion flows from heart to heart was driven home to Paul when his mother passed away. He observed that people displayed various levels of responses to her passing. One level was that he simply didn't hear from some folks. No response at all. Others might say, "Oh yeah, heard about your mother—really sorry"—and that was the extent of their sympathy. That group was too busy to bother doing more. At another level, Paul would receive cards from people who took the time and energy to share their sadness or their sense of thinking about him, which he appreciated. And then there was the occasional communication that was so genuine, so authentic, and so much at the heart level that it moved Paul deeply. It wasn't a matter of intellectual sharing—rather, it was the emotional connection that was created. We believe that true compassion is about making an emotional connection with people in a time of need in such a way that they get it and feel the connection. This extraordinarily powerful link has to do with your willingness to be open to other people and to care enough about others to share that sense with them.

When you feel a sense of compassion, or when something comes into your consciousness that triggers such feelings or thoughts, what do you do? That feeling has to become a trigger that prompts you to stop and reorder your priorities so that you can act on that sense of compassion you're experiencing. It's a reminder to make room in your life and make time to express it. Otherwise (and this happens all too frequently), we may say to ourselves, "Oh, I'll deal with that later." And then later becomes later and even later, which often becomes never. When we experience that sense of compassion, we should try to act on it before the feeling escapes us. You have to be active to show compassion—it's not a passive quality.

Ways in Which Leaders Nurture and Uplift Others

To nurture someone is to provide them with what they need at a particular moment. Nurturing can take many different forms. It can mean being very supportive emotionally. It can mean providing people with the right structure or the right set of challenges to confront in order to make them stronger and allow them to grow. It can mean providing a safe place for people to fall so that they don't hurt themselves. Wise leaders have the ability to nurture individuals, groups, and entire organizations—nurture in the sense of providing the right conditions for individuals, groups, and organizations to grow, and grow in a way that's healthy and that supports a positive evolutionary path.

Uplifting, on the other hand, is helping people move toward their highest potential and showing them the way forward. It means providing a pathway to their higher potential, and then doing whatever is necessary to uplift them along the way, in order to put the wind under their wings so that they can take advantage of that uplift.

As to uplifting others, one of Steve's mentors used to say that every time you come in contact with another human being, what you choose to say to him can either enhance or diminish his self-esteem. Taking advantage of the opportunity to enhance the way another person sees himself or herself is one way in which wise leaders uplift others continually.

Wise leaders leverage the power of expectations and belief. Believing in people's potential and believing that they really are capable—capable of growing, capable of handling responsibility, capable of doing difficult things—helps uplift them because they then see themselves through your eyes. And if your eyes reflect a new and improved version of the other person, or the next evolution of that person in a positive way, he begins to see himself in that image and move toward it. Uplifting can be a very natural phenomenon that occurs simply because you look at another human being and see that person in a positive light.

Sometimes, when we look at the person sitting across the desk from us, we realize that he can do and be more than what we are seeing at that moment. Paul recalls struggling constantly with some staff members to help them understand that people are unfinished creatures—that God isn't through with us yet. We are constantly growing and expanding, and we are not as good today as we will be tomorrow. One of the roles of the wise leader is to help others understand that truth, and to be supportive of the process of trying to uplift fellow humans who aren't yet where they need to be.

Creating Climates and Cultures That Bring Out the Best in People

Wise leaders create climates and cultures that bring out the best in people. Wise leaders delegate, stretching people by giving them increased responsibilities and increased opportunities to shine. But they must be willing to pick people up and dust them off when they fall down, patching them up and telling them, "It's going to be okay. It's going to be better. You're going to survive and be able to move forward."

To gain a perspective on organizational cultures that bring out the best in people, we recommend Richard Farson's wonderful book, *Whoever Makes the Most Mistakes Wins*. Farson helps us understand that mistakes and success are tied together. Sometimes you can't distinguish between them and often one leads to the other. What may look like a mistake today may be the precursor of a wonderful success tomorrow. Or what may look like a success today could be the beginning of tomorrow's downfall. The wise leader creates an atmosphere that tells employees, "We're not going to sweat the difficulties; we're going to make sure that we move past them to that next opportunity to succeed." It is the leader's responsibility to create the sense of freedom that allows people to succeed, or to fail. People can be hobbled by fear in the absence of a climate that allows them to feel free enough and safe enough to be who they really are, to bring their gifts forward, and to try new things, knowing that sometimes their ideas will work and sometimes they won't.

As wise leaders we know that the culture we create—one that brings out the best in people—usually has a component calling for continued investment in others' growth. Most organizations accomplish that investment in growth through professional development, or by providing growth experiences or opportunities to attend conferences, or by opportunities to perform more challenging tasks—all of which help people to see that they are appreciated and respected. When we invest in people they are more likely to invest in themselves.

Leaders bring out the best in people by giving them the resources needed to show their creativity, their originality, and their initiative, because without those resources they may be stymied or stifled. Wise leaders also help people to find ways in which a particular assignment can be aligned with what they're good at, or with their next career step.

Creating Programs and Structures That Bring Out the Best in People

One factor that leaders can influence and control is the organizational structures in which people work. There are collaborative structures as well as structures that are very control oriented and hierarchically arranged. The nature of the structure determines the way people relate to each other. Do you have groups of people who by title and function are expected to meet and collaborate as a part of their job? Or is the organization structured so that each person is expected to work mostly on an individual basis, with minimal collaboration?

We have seen tremendous differences occur in organizations as a result of changing some aspect of the organizational structure. For example, one structural change could be creating a common meeting time to facilitate collaboration. Steve recalls a situation in one district where he served as superintendent that required regular classroom teachers and special education teachers to work together in the same classroom. However, the two groups of teachers had different planning periods, different lunch schedules, and different after-school responsibilities. Despite their differing philosophies and teaching styles, they had a shared responsibility for teaching the same special-needs children in a regular classroom setting. A great deal of confusion, as well as anger and frustration, arose concerning respective roles and responsibilities. It was like having two cooks in the same kitchen! Through the negotiated contract with the teacher union, Steve arranged a structural change that set aside a regular common meeting time that allowed these teachers to collaborate. This single change energized people by enabling them to support each other rather than to continue working at cross-purposes.

Creating structures that make it possible for people to be successful is a form of compassion that allows people to do their best and to fulfill their potential. In this case, not only did the teachers benefit, but so did the children. Without the opportunity for collaboration, very different outcomes result.

The same thing happens with regard to programs. Most organizations have programs of various kinds, whether they're operating procedures, training programs, or delivery systems. All such aspects of organizational life can be created in a way that either brings out the best in people or stifles them. If the existing structures routinely give people less time than is really needed to perform a task, they are going to fail. So wise leaders have a responsibility to think programmatically *and* structurally about what people need and how to bring people together in their work environment in a way that will enable them to be and do their best.

Many years ago Alvin Toffler, in his powerful book *Future Shock,* wrote about the idea of "adhocracy" as opposed to bureaucracy—that is, creating flexible organizational charts that could be reconfigured continually depending on a particular initiative and crossing traditional line-and-staff hierarchical relationships. Leaders need to be creative in finding ways to put people together in novel configurations that allow each person to bring his or her unique perspective to that particular process.

Wise Leaders Modify Rules to Better Meet People's Needs

Some degree of structure is needed in any organization in order for people to be happy. Standard operating procedures, policies, and codes of conduct are important—but so is flexibility! Sometimes compassion argues in favor of forgiving a rule or even ignoring it altogether. How many hours a week does someone work? If someone has worked very hard and even put in extra time, why not look the other way some day when he needs to go home early because his parents are visiting from out of town? The personnel manual may say, "You can't do that," but compassion would say, "Yeah, that's the right way to go." Flexibility becomes an important consideration in terms of human needs. And it probably goes without saying that you refuse to bend the rules for someone who continually tries to take advantage of the system by cutting corners and shirking responsibilities.

Wise leaders look at the circumstances and then figure out how to respond to people's needs. Wise leaders individualize whenever they can, but they do so in an even-handed and fair manner. Rules may work generally, but there are situations that warrant exceptions, when we must use our judgment to be flexible, in order to do the right thing.

We are *not* suggesting modifying rules arbitrarily without a reason. We're talking about being better able to meet the needs of the people in your organization. When you bend a rule and people know that you're bending a rule for them under legitimate circumstances, our experience has been that they will bend over backward to justify your faith in them. Rather than taking advantage of such flexibility, over time, employees tend to pay back the organization many-fold.

Steve recalls an instance when a staff member asked if she could take a computer home to work on a given project. She had to be at home to accept delivery of an appliance, but the nature of her work that day could just as easily be performed away from the office. Steve was aware that this person did not make a habit of such requests; in fact, this was the first such request she had made in the five years she had worked for him. The result was that she accomplished more that day at home than she might have at the office—possibly because she felt the need to justify Steve's faith in her.

The moral: although every rule has some underlying purpose, there are times when that rule must be tempered or set aside for a greater good that becomes apparent from a larger perspective. There may also be times when such an exception cannot be made officially because of a concern that others will try to use it to set a precedent. Instead, "a wink and a nod" will suffice.

We also appreciate the old saying that "Sometimes it's better to ask forgiveness than to ask permission." And sometimes it's better to give forgiveness than it is to give permission. Wise leaders understand when and how to make such judgments. These kinds of circumstances call for good judgment and a readiness to explain why you do what you do. When you're doing the right thing and appropriately bending otherwise rigid rules for people, they will perceive you as being a compassionate leader, because you are.

Wise Leaders Show Special Sensitivity When People Are Coping with Severe Hardships

Wise leaders understand that situations change and circumstances change. The person who's not at his best this week or this month because he's going through a difficult time may be the critical person in your organization a year from now, and may be the difference between the organization's success or failure. Life has its own rhythms—and those rhythms are subject to continual changes. Some days you're up and some days you're down. When you bring people into your organization, you have a similar understanding: that they will have ups and downs, and they deserve the same kind of support when they're down as you will give them when they are contributing more fully.

Several years ago one of Paul's valued employees became ill and was not functioning well. He was virtually useless at work. The consensus among Paul's senior staff members was, "Well, he has devoted so much to the organization that we owe it to him to stand by him and not discard him." The employee finally changed doctors and began taking a different medication. Although he lost about a hundred pounds, he was transformed from being nonfunctional to being quite valuable to the organization and eventually recaptured and even improved on the kinds of contributions he had made prior to his illness.

In any organization it's inevitable that some people will be faced with a personal tragedy or a severe hardship. Steve dealt with numerous examples of employees who had a terminal illness but who had used all their sick leave, or an employee whose contract was not being renewed but who was seriously ill and would lose paid health benefits when their contract expired. In such cases, Steve always figured out a way to act with compassion by granting additional sick leave, or by extending a contract for several months, or by paying all or part of a health insurance premium even though he wasn't required to do so. In some of those cases, he had the authority as a superintendent to make such accommodations. But when certain situations required the approval of the school board, invariably the board would respond with compassion, going above and beyond what was required to assist someone through a personal tragedy or severe hardship.

Sometimes a leader will manage matters in a most discreet way in order to protect the dignity and privacy of the person in need. Even so, there are times when others in the organization become aware that a kindness has been extended to one of their colleagues. That sends an important message: "Who knows what the future may hold, but I now know that if I have a personal tragedy or hardship, I work in an organization whose leaders are caring and compassionate and that in all likelihood they will be there for me as well." The way in which such life-changing circumstances are handled has a powerful effect on the way people feel about their organization, and the leaders for whom they work.

Compassionate Acts Are Long Remembered and Appreciated

Compassionate acts tend to engender deep feelings of appreciation. During times when people are hurting, in need, and vulnerable, they are acutely sensitive to expressions of compassion. When you as the leader reach out in a compassionate way to people during those times, your response is long remembered. Life in a school district, or in any organization, is replete with opportunities for us, as leaders, to act with compassion. Never underestimate the lasting power of those acts and their ripple effects.

One week after starting a new teaching job, Steve's wife was diagnosed with breast cancer. After consulting her doctor, she decided that six weeks of radiation therapy was the best treatment option and that her sense of hope and well-being would be best served if she could continue teaching half-time during the therapy. She planned to teach in the morning and receive treatment each afternoon. Her principal, the personnel director, and the superintendent all agreed that they would approve her request for six weeks of sick leave on a half-time basis if she was physically able to meet her teaching responsibilities. The school leaders felt that having the same teacher for the entire year—though only half-time for six weeks—would also best serve the children as well as the teacher. Twenty-five years later neither Steve nor his wife Laney has forgotten the compassion of those leaders at that difficult time. They could just as easily have refused Laney's request, and her hopeful, positive attitude might well have been extinguished.

Many similar situations present themselves in any organization, and leaders have the opportunity to respond with or without compassion. The way in which these deeply personal situations are handled is long remembered, and they affect the way we view our leaders and employers. Were they there for you when you needed them, or do you work in a place that's cold and hard and unbending in times of human need?

Compassion has the power to create permanent connections. It becomes an authentic binder between people. Often an act of compassion creates a lifelong friendship or relationship. Sometimes your interaction with another person registers deep within you; you know in your heart that you are experiencing a true, totally authentic moment. Such a rare experience creates not just a memory, but also a desire to get closer and stay closer to the person with whom you have shared the moment. There are so few of these kinds of moments in anyone's life; when one presents itself to you, the natural feeling is to want to form a lasting relationship with the person who shared it. The more a leader can behave in that authentic way, leading from his or her heart, the greater the likelihood of building strong bonds with his or her coworkers.

Opportunities for compassion abound. As a superintendent, Steve faithfully took the time to send handwritten sympathy notes to people on his staff who had lost someone. Consequently, people would come up to him, months later, to extend thanks for taking the time to write a note, or for attending the viewing or funeral of a loved one. He remembers when one of his building principals was undergoing a catheterization procedure and an angioplasty. The exams took place on a weekend, and in a hospital that was not nearby. Steve chose to be there when the principal came out of the recovery room. The principal was deeply touched by Steve's act of caring; he told Steve how much his visit meant. That compassionate act helped create a bond between Steve and this principal that has lasted twenty years.

Whenever possible, wise leaders take the time to attend viewings and funerals, to call and ask how someone is doing following an accident or a surgery or an illness, or to send a note of concern or condolence. Knowing that life is fraught with hardship, illness, tragedies, and death, wise leaders show their compassion in ways large and small.

Compassion Is the Golden Rule in Action

All of us, regardless of our age or station in life, desire to be treated with compassion. If that's the way we wish to be treated, however, we need to model such actions ourselves. The part of the Golden Rule that says "as you would have others do unto you" is not intended to make others feel obligated to do good things for you; it's to help *you* know the right thing to do for others.

As leaders, we make many decisions amid circumstances that are not clear-cut, circumstances that force us to make close calls, tough calls. Often it's not readily apparent what is the right thing to do in a given situation. Wise leaders take the time to project themselves into the other person's shoes, asking, "How would I want to be treated? What would I think would be fair? What would I see as compassionate?"

Even if we feel the impulse to act compassionately, we may not be entirely clear about the most compassionate choice. In some cases a kick in the pants may actually be more compassionate than a kind word. Putting yourself mentally into another's situation may help you see a compassionate course of action that is wise, not just sentimental. Real compassion takes the whole picture into account in choosing the wisest course.

When Steve was in high school, he worked as a counselor at a camp for physically handicapped children. One of the campers had done a sloppy job of making his bed. Steve insisted sternly that the boy make his bed as camp rules specified. A visitor who had observed the situation and had seen the boy crying, later asked Steve how he could be so cruel.

The visitor said, "That boy can't even stand up without his braces and crutches!"

Steve replied, "The difference between you and me is that I know he can make his bed as well as any of the other children; it will just take him longer. If our cabin loses points during inspection because of his sloppy bed, the other campers will take it out on him. In this cabin he will learn that if he puts forth the effort, he can be as successful as any of the other campers." When the boy remade his bed, he did it correctly; his crocodile tears quickly faded, giving way to a sense of satisfaction and a sincere smile.

Steve's discipline didn't look like a compassionate act unless you had the proper lens and could see it from the vantage point of its ultimate positive effect on the camper involved. Wise leaders see themselves in the other person's shoes and then act with true compassion.

To become The Wise Leader:

- Operate from a base of compassion.
- Nurture and uplift others.
- Create climates and cultures that bring out the best in people.
- Create programs and structures that bring out the best in people.
- Modify rules to better meet the needs of people.
- Show a special sensitivity when people are coping with severe hardships or personal tragedies.
- Engender loyalty and appreciation by being compassionate.
- Know compassion is the Golden Rule in action.

CHAPTER 16

The Wisdom of Hope over Fear

Hope and fear are closely interrelated. The more of one we feel, the less of the other is possible. Weak leaders use fear as a tool or weapon to maintain control. Wise leaders, on the other hand, understand that hope is their strongest tool. They believe in themselves and their own potential for growth, and they build on this hope to develop their people and their organization. They believe that circumstances and people can be better than they are. They believe that the world can be a better place than it is. They see things not just as they are, but as they could be. Because they see and believe this so strongly, they engender hope in others.

Wise leaders empower people. They energize them and give wings to their hopes and dreams. They do this by creating an environment and culture that allows people to feel secure and free to dream—free to develop their own unique gifts and talents, and with the belief that they can put their gifts and talents to good use. By helping others fulfill their dreams wise leaders help to propel the world toward a brighter future.

Their integrity and positive attitude toward life allows wise leaders not only to create trust and hope but also to diminish fear. In the presence of a wise leader hope expands and fear contracts. Wise leaders starve fear and feed hope. Although fear is a natural and sometimes even helpful emotion that can keep us from doing stupid things or taking risks beyond our capacity, it can also incapacitate us. An appropriate amount of fear can teach us to respect challenging situations and act accordingly. Fear run amok within us can become debilitating and corrosive. Wise leaders help people confront and overcome their fears. In the midst of chaotic and confusing situations, wise leaders know how to step back and see the world from a detached perspective. Wise leaders learn how to keep their egos in check and to see things holistically. They learn how to keep their own fear in check so that they can reassure others. From that perspective they can find a path through chaotic and difficult terrain.

Wise leaders understand and find the right balance between freedom and control in their organizations. They understand that organizations are best served when the reins of control are held lightly. They understand that pulling on the reins too hard can cause things to come to a screeching stop.

Keeping balance is always a challenge. Wise leaders understand both the necessity of balance and how very difficult balance can be to achieve and maintain. Leaders must be sufficiently detached to view things with perspective, but not so detached as to be remote and uncaring. Wise leaders are confident yet humble, thick-skinned but empathetic. They understand that the need for control must be balanced with the right amount of freedom. They understand that they must work constantly to diminish fear so that hope can grow.

Engendering Hope in Others

Before creating hope in others, a leader must have a sense of hope himself. Leaders who lack any sense of possibility are the worst kind of leaders. Wise leaders understand that things can and will be better. Like Annie in the musical, they know in their hearts that the sun will come out tomorrow. But first and foremost they always hold that belief for themselves. You cannot invoke something in others that you don't possess yourself. "Do as I say, not as I do" doesn't cut it. Leaders are role models. What they demonstrate on a daily basis is what others emulate. Wise leaders are "potentialists." They see the possibility in what can be and refuse to be constrained by what is. Wise leaders are "hope pushers," and they believe in what they are selling to others. Wise leaders are drawn to a positive vision of things and the energy associated with that vision. Such leaders are not wishers who look to the stars for help; they know that anything worth creating is difficult. But they also believe that the change that comes along with their vision is possible because they believe in the positive potential in people, both individually and collectively. Wise leaders do not see the future as something that might be; they see it as what is now only partially fulfilled, the rest depending on planning and effort. Because they know this, they have the power to create a sense of excitement and positive energy. Others pick up on this energy and experience it as hope.

Wise leaders not only have the ability to see the future—they *believe* in the future they see. That's the difference between dreamers and doers. Dreamers can see what might be. Doers get it done. A leader who truly sees and believes in possibility can communicate that possibility to others so that others come to believe it too. At first, followers must borrow hope from the leader, but as progress is made they too come to own it. First they believe in the leader, then they come to believe in what the leader believes, and then they come to believe in themselves.

Leaders Must Help Others Fulfill Their Hopes and Dreams

Wise leaders give wings to the hopes and dreams of others. Here is the heart of leadership. Wise leaders take people to places they may only have dreamed of—and sometimes they take them to places they never dared to dream about. True leaders create a sense of possibility in others. They create conditions that allow others to feel free to dream and to begin to express that dream. Wise leaders create an environment in which an open discussion of possibilities occurs regularly. Such discussions allow the leader to knit the various individual dreams together into a tapestry that serves the broader purpose of the organization.

Many years ago one of Steve's staff members asked for a computer in his classroom so he could use it for instruction. (This was well before computers in classrooms were common.) He told Steve of his grand plans for that computer. Steve suggested that he prepare a proposal—not just for a single computer, but for a whole computer lab. That lab became the beginning of a network that served the entire district. That one teacher's dream, enabled by the leader, created a reality that affected many others. When you listen to and understand people's dreams, you understand who they are and what they might become. In understanding that teacher's dream, Steve set in force a multiplier effect that affected the entire district.

When Paul visits other countries he always asks the people he meets about their dreams. He has found that the answers he receives tell him a lot about the country he's visiting. If the dreams are small and cramped, then the freedom to be and to dream is small and cramped. When people's dreams are bigger and grander the possibility of what that country can become is similarly more expansive. Without the freedom to dream, you lack the most basic freedom. The same is true for organizations: leaders should constantly be asking themselves, "What kinds of dreams are we having in this organization?"

Dreams live at the core of our souls. They are what our souls wake up to. When dreams abound with hope and possibility the soul soars. When dreams are limited and compressed the soul can wither. Your dreams should match your capacity. When you have great capacity you must dream big—and when you dream big, if you're willing to put the work behind your dream, your capacity will be magnified.

During a conversation with one of America's leading technological entrepreneurs, Paul inquired about the man's dreams. Faster computing was the response. (To be generous, speed was only part of a much greater dream of networking the world and making technology ubiquitous.) Later in the same conversation the business giant returned to that dream and admitted that he had achieved most of his goals much faster and earlier than he had ever imagined possible and that he needed to reconsider his dreams. The happy ending here is that he has since used the wealth generated from his faster computers to help the world in a number of ways. He started dreaming up to his capacity.

The ability to dream and hope is really an expression of our higher selves, our connection to what is best in us. Sadly, many situations exist in which economics or other societal and environmental factors make it hard for people to entertain hope. What kind of wreckage does that create with their higher selves?

Leaders Must Understand the Relationship between Fear and Trust

Trust underlies the possibility of hope. People must trust in the leader and the leader must trust in his people for there to be any hope whatsoever. It's difficult to separate trust from hope. And it's also hard to separate trust from fear because trust and fear are two ends of the same seesaw. When one goes up, the other goes down. The more trust you have, the less fear you feel. The more fearful you are, the less trusting you are.

The role of the wise leader is to increase trust and diminish fear. Those inside your circle tend to be those whom you trust. Those outside the circle are those you fear to some degree. Wise leaders work on broadening the circle and increasing the level of trust so that fear is diminished.

Some level of fear can protect us. But trouble starts when fear begins to produce a debilitating effect. We must teach young children that fire burns and knives cut, but we don't want them to think that everything they might touch is hot or sharp. A sense of balance is needed. Fear may not be exactly the right word for the healthy side of seeing dangers; Paul has always preferred the word "respect." When he travels to a new and perhaps strange place he tries to be respectful of whatever environment he finds himself in. If it's reputed to be dangerous he tries to go out with others, for instance, or he tries to avoid certain areas that might be more dangerous. He tries not to be provocative in word or deed. This is showing a proper respect for the environment. We must respect the dangers of the world but still be willing to walk in it. When you're walking down a dark street at night, don't be so naïve as to think nothing bad can possibly happen to you. Do take the occasional glance over your shoulder to see if something threatening might be looming. If you spend all your time looking back over your shoulder, however, you risk walking into a wall. Again, balance is important!

Some hold the belief that animals can smell fear. When we are fearful, somehow we give off energy that can escalate whatever situation is causing us fear. Then we are creating a self-fulfilling cycle. This "fear energy" gives power to the very forces that created it. "Never let them see you sweat," some executives maintain. *We* believe when you let fear overcome you, you make things worse.

In an idyllic world there would be no need for fear because there would be no threats. We are a long way from that paradise. So until nirvana comes, we must learn and teach a healthy respect for what could happen. Meanwhile, wise leaders can work to diminish fear by increasing the level of trust that both leader and followers feel.

Overcoming Our Fear

Sometimes the best way to overcome fear is to take an existential leap toward trust. It's necessary for us to understand that fear *will* limit us and our possibilities. One place to start overcoming our fears is to sort things out in a rational way. You can say, "I'm afraid a meteor will destroy the earth," but the odds aren't great that will happen anytime soon, and there's little we could do about such a cataclysm anyway. You can also say, "I'm afraid I'll get cancer." That fear is more plausible, but by choosing a healthier lifestyle and getting regular examinations you might lessen its likelihood. One way to overcome fear is to act on the things you *can* act on—to figure out which of the things you fear have actionable responses.

In his well-traveled life Paul has run into many frustrating and difficult situations. His first response is always to ask himself, "Is this something I can do something about? Okay, my flight is cancelled. Are other flights available? Are *all* the flights cancelled because of weather? If so, that doesn't seem to be worthy of worry." In such a case, let the people who are expecting you know what's going on and that you'll be on your way as soon as possible.

We must constantly ask ourselves what we can change and what we can't. We need to take on those things that are changeable and to accept the others. The well-known prayer that originated with the theologian Reinhold Niebuhr tells us: "Grant me the serenity to accept the things I cannot change, the courage to change the things I can, and wisdom to know the difference." This is excellent advice for the wise leader who wishes to face fear and create trust.

Most of us have known people who faced serious health issues or the possibility of serious issues. Those who had the courage and the willpower were able to change their lifestyles to improve their chances of avoiding further problems. Others simply ignored them or failed to muster the courage to change.

One of the most powerful ways in which we can face our fears is to express them openly. Keeping your fears to yourself creates an internal loop that seems to give the fear more power. Expressing your fear diminishes its power over you. Steve's mother used to tell him, "There's more room on the outside than the inside." (More proof, if it's needed, of how wise our mothers can be.) She understood that things kept inside fester and grow. Releasing them gives them space to dissipate and dissolve. Fear is like a shadow that seems bigger and scarier than it really is. Exposed to sunlight, it can be seen for what it is—it seems smaller. Mark Twain once said, "Worry is interest paid in advance for trouble that never happens." That's what fear is. Obviously the things that we worry about are sometimes all too real and really do happen. None of our worrying had the power to stop such occurrences, however. The Bible reminds us that even as we walk through the valley of the shadow of death, we need fear no evil. In biblical terms, evil and bad exist, but they are not things that should deter us.

Fear can inhibit and inhabit our mind, our body, and our spirit. Our fears have the power to bring about physical and spiritual effects in us. Our body stores fears and patterns. If we experience pain someplace in our body, we tend to favor that part and in some cases we begin to lose the use of it. As we become more incapacitated, fear takes its toll on our spirit and our view of the world. This is also true for organizations. During financial recessions we see people become more fearful of their finances; they start cutting back on their spending, creating a lack of demand that tends to curtail the business cycle even further, creating a deepening problem.

Sometimes we have to overcome our fear simply by acknowledging it and moving forward. Once Steve found that his TV antenna had stopped working properly. He decided to go up on the roof to fix it. As he climbed the ladder, what had seemed to be a good idea became less appealing with each step. When he got to the top he realized that it looked a lot higher from the top than it did when he was standing safely on the ground. Fear began to grip him so that he could barely move. He decided to pause for a moment and take a look around. Suddenly Steve realized that, because he was looking at everything from on high, he had gained a perspective of his house and the neighborhood never available to him before. He started to see the beauty all around him. He was still afraid, but he did some self-talk about the reality that he really could do what he had set out to do and he made his way to the damaged antenna. Unfortunately, he couldn't fix it—but now he has cable and doesn't have to worry about it! He also has the power that comes from having faced and overcome his fear.

We have within us the power to cut fear down to size. In Steve's case, he reframed it by trading his fear for an appreciation of the beauty of the day and the fresh perspective of a different viewpoint. In the wonderful movie *Dead Poets Society,* the teacher, played by Robin Williams, had his students stand on their desks so they could see the world from a different perspective. Wise leaders constantly provide fresh perspectives for themselves and others.

Obviously, those who have faith also have a powerful weapon against fear. Their belief that a greater power is on their side gives them a sense of hope. Early in Paul's career as a public school superintendent he had a board member who was truly awful. Not only was she dishonest, but she was a bully who tried to control everything and everyone. Paul's contract was coming up for renewal, and this woman had made it clear that she wanted to have him fired because he had not let her have her way with the district. He felt certain that she was willing to fabricate and exaggerate lies about him, creating a huge problem. Paul realized that he was becoming increasingly consumed by this issue and by her threat to uproot him and his family. He felt as if his whole life screen were filled with this woman's face. She was a constant source of worry and torment for him. One Sunday he prayed to God, saying, "You're going to have to handle this for me, Lord. I can't do it." At that moment he felt almost a physical whooshing sound, like a balloon deflating, and with that feeling the big balloon of her face in his vision became smaller and smaller until she occupied only a little corner of his "screen." She was still a problem for Paul, but he realized that she was a little problem and he would feed her energy no more. Peace washed over him and the sun came out again.

Acting on a sense of faith in a higher power, Paul surrendered his fears to it. Not everyone has a religious perspective that allows for this kind of action, but we all have the ability to make the wise choice between what we can change and what we can't and the ability to put things into perspective. People and organizations are best served when we allow the power of our hopes to trump our fears.

Clearly, religion in all forms provides a sense of comfort and strength for a great many people. For Christians there is so much around the issue of "fearing not" and trusting in God, whose power can overcome your problems. So clearly one path to overcoming fear is through prayer or faith in a greater power. But for those who are not believers another greater power is also available: the power of working with others. In the M. Night Shyamalan movie *Signs* we see an invasion of earth by alien beings. The movie raises the question, "Are we alone?" At one level it's a question of whether we exist in this universe as a lone species or if there are others out there. At another level, the movie raises the question of whether we are alone or if a higher power is looking after us. At the most basic level, however, the answer to the question of whether we are alone is a resounding "No"—because we have each other. We gain strength from those around us, which is why a leader who can unite an organization to work toward common needs and ends can be so powerful.

Sadly, too many leaders try to use fear as a galvanizing force to create a sense of togetherness. They create or point to an external enemy to be resisted or overcome. Or they use division to weaken those with whom they work so that they can maintain the upper hand. Perhaps one of the most common tactics of fear-inducing leaders is their use of intimidation or punitive accountability. Wise leaders try to bring people together and make them feel safe. They work to empower others, not to make them afraid.

Reducing Fear in Your Organization

The first way to reduce fear, of course, is not to create it in the first place. Wise leaders know that fear-inducing strategies only weaken the organization, and ultimately the leader's credibility and strength. They don't try to divide or create false fears or intimidate. Moreover, wise leaders realize that everything they do is magnified. What seems like a small gesture to the leader resonates like thunder to those below them in the organization. The modeling you do is always under close scrutiny.

It's all too easy to induce fear without meaning to do so if you are unaware that your actions may have disproportionately negative consequences. Ironically, one of the most important things a leader can do is to be honest with staff members. But honesty can also create great fear. If the organization is facing a budget crisis, for instance, sharing information about the crisis can create a concomitant fear of job loss or other uncertainties. Still, the best solution is not to hide important information. Leaders must decide, honestly with themselves, what information is important to hold back and what is important to share. When bad news must be shared, it should be supplemented with genuine caring and reassurance. Leaders can reduce fear by the subtle positive things they say and do, because that also will be magnified.

The expression of clarity and hope can soothe fears in an organization. If a budget problem causes people to be fearful of losing their jobs, talk to them about what kinds of things might be done without resorting to cutbacks in staff. Paul once found it necessary to freeze salaries and benefits for a period of time. But he assured staff members that, when budgets matters improved, they would share in the benefits by getting their raises and better benefits. He was able to keep his word to the staff as the situation improved, and that gave him greater credibility the next time a problem arose. People in the organization were much less fearful because they knew he would talk to them honestly and act fairly.

People will always look to the leader for clues and cues about what is happening and how things are going. Wise leaders stay positive and give off an air of confidence and belief because that is the core of who they are. Leaders who have consistently displayed a strong relationship between what they say and what they do—who have shown integrity, in other words—will be trusted. Wise leaders let people know that they have a plan to handle difficult situations; whenever possible, people within the organization should be included in the planning process. Inclusion allows people to feel ownership of the solution and to feel empowered rather than victimized. Fear paralyzes, but ownership diminishes fear. The antidote to paralysis is action and movement. You begin to dispel fear by not acting afraid. When Steve stepped out onto his roof he didn't really feel terribly brave, but as he acted on his need for bravery it came to him. Taking action allows you to feel a sense of forward progress, which allays fear.

Mastering the Art of Detachment

Always remember that attachment in a positive situation has great power. Naturally you feel a sense of attachment to those whom you love and who love you. But it is crucial to learn to separate those things that require attachment from those that require detachment. It's always good to have some emotional connection to people and events, but a wise leader guards against becoming overly attached emotionally to what's going on. Wise leaders find ways of stepping back and creating some distance between their emotions and what's happening around them.

One of pro basketball's greatest coaches, Phil Jackson, winner of eleven NBA titles, is famous for his detached style of coaching. He credits much of his detachment to his study of Zen Buddhism. If you observed him on the bench, even when the game seemed out of control, you'd see him smiling. Why? Because he felt serene in the moment and confident of his abilities to fix whatever needed fixing. He didn't let momentary setbacks hold any power over him. He understood the flow of life around him. He was also known for being able to handle some of basketball's greatest superstars—and largest egos. He didn't engage any of his players in a battle of wills; he knew he was in charge and he knew what battles to fight. And he was able to bring his players along with him.

During one particular game when things were going badly, Jackson called a time-out. The team gathered around him to learn how he wanted them to improve the situation. But Jackson turned his back on the players and said nothing. As the time-out was about to end, one player said, "Oh, I get it—he told us what to do at the last time-out and we haven't done it yet." Jackson turned around and smiled at the players as they returned to the floor and did what he had originally expected. Now there's real detachment.

When you cannot detach yourself, those things to which you're attached hold power over you. The board member with whom Paul had problems had become an overwhelming and terribly unwelcome presence in his life—she was with him in thought morning, noon, and night. It was only when he learned to detach himself from her and his fear of what she could do to him that he found peace. Wise leaders work on finding ways to create detachment from the emotional situations that surround them. They should feel for them, but not be driven by them. There is, of course, the danger of too much detachment. When you no longer connect or feel at all, you are useless as a leader. It's good to remember to balance the head and the heart and to remember that the "head bone" is connected to the "heart bone."

Leaders Must Not Hold the Reins of Control Too Tightly

Too much control reduces people's freedom to dream. Any kind of control, even if benignly intended, is an imposition of one person's will and vision on another. When a child is growing up, the parent tends to impose his will and vision on the child with the aim of providing a framework of understanding of how to proceed in life. Ideally, as a child matures the parent steps back and provides more space and freedom. When the child reaches adulthood, a parent should try to develop a relationship that is loving and supportive but also somewhat detached from the child's everyday existence, allowing the child to live an independent, mature life. A parent who behaves toward the adult child in the same way as when the child was young does not allow the child to grow and blossom. Similarly, the ancient Chinese practice of binding a young female child's feet prevented girls from learning to walk because their feet became stunted and useless. When a leader binds people through overzealous control, the organization will suffer.

The only sure way to establish very tight control is through fear and intimidation. Show us an organization that is not growing and flowing, one in which people behave in a rigid and controlled manner, and we'll show you an organization built on fear. Tight control sets the stage for dysfunction and dissatisfaction. If people are able to leave, they will do so. (This is why staying aware of the rate of attrition in an organization is useful.) In difficult times, however, when fewer options are available, employees will tend to stay physically but leave psychologically, and they'll often wage a form of guerilla warfare inside the organization because of their unhappiness.

A leader who is willing to live with a minimal response of compliance in an organization will be quite willing to exert control through fear. If the organization is to flourish, though, intimidation will not work. People cannot be bludgeoned into greatness or beaten into excellence. External control can control people's actions, but not their heads and hearts. When a leader can affirm and uplift people and let them go where their heads and hearts take them, then the organization will thrive.

A wise leader holds the reins of the organization loosely so it can gather speed. When the reins are held too tightly on a horse, it will slow down and eventually stop; it might even rear up and try to throw the rider. The same is true of people. When the reins are gripped too tightly people will also slow down or ultimately rebel. When the reins are loosened, however, people, like horses, will run like the wind. A wise leader holds the reins loosely. Such leaders are still in control of the direction being taken and can also affect the speed of the journey. When the leader is certain of the proper course and the pace, then the grip on the reins can be relaxed once more.

Beware of Wanting Something Too Much or Holding It Too Tightly

Once a wise old man was holding forth before a group of townspeople. A brash young man, not impressed by the sage's wisdom, decided to embarrass him before everyone. He approached the old man holding a bird in his hand and asked the wise man if the bird was alive or dead. If the old man said the bird was alive, the younger man planned to squeeze it to death. If the sage said it was dead, the young man would open his hands and let the bird fly away. Either way, he thought, he would show the townsfolk that he was smarter than the wise old man. When he asked the old man if the bird he was holding was alive or dead, the wise man replied quite simply, "The answer to that is in your hands."

A leader who tries to grip the reins too tightly poses grave danger to an organization. That kind of leader may squeeze the life out of it. Instead, sometimes the best course of action is to try to create the conditions for what you want to see happen and then step back and see how things evolve. This is true in both organizations and personal relations. As the old saying tell us, "If you love something, let it go." If it comes back, it is yours; if it doesn't, it never was yours.

Wise leaders understand that there are seasons to a life, an organization, or a business. Sometimes it is the right time to move; at other times it is the right time to hold back. Paul and Steve once were told by an exceedingly wise professor that there is a very thin line between belief and obsession. Learning to let go becomes vitally important. Life itself is impermanent and will end at some point. Holding on to things to the point of obsession doesn't serve us well. Overattachment creates rigidity, whereas wise leaders strive for flexibility.

We know, at some level, that our children come through us but are not us. They are loaned to us for a while and our task is to raise them the best we can and then let them soar. The same is true for organizations. Even if you technically "own" the organization, it is, at best, on loan to you. You will not take it with you into the next life. The world lets us know when we have been holding on to things too tightly—and that's not usually a pleasant experience.

Part of creating a balance in our lives is to look at events with the long run in mind. If you do that, you understand that trying to hold on to something in the moment makes no sense. You become enslaved by what you're trying to hold on to.

Both Steve and Paul have visited the ruins of the ancient cities in Israel. For millennia each new city was built upon the ruins of the previous city. The cities were walled cities and the very act of building a wall around the city limited its growth and its ability to change with time. The only way the cities could grow was to be destroyed so that new cities could be built upon the ruins. This is also true of our fears. Our fears build walls around us and stunt our ability to grow. Walls keep people out, but they also keep people in. Wise leaders don't build walls around their people; they teach them how to run free.

To become The Wise Leaders:

- Engender a sense of hope in others.
- Help others fulfill their hopes and dreams.
- See how others' hopes and dreams fit into the larger mosaic.
- Understand the relationship between fear and trust.
- Know how to respond to fear and overcome it.
- Know how to reduce fear in your organization.
- Understand the difference between a detached perspective and not caring.
- Know how to modulate the reins of control.
- Guard against becoming overly attached to people or circumstances.

CHAPTER 17

The Wisdom of Love

It may seem strange to include a chapter about love in a book about leadership, but this book deals with wise leadership and the underlying archetypal values that engender wisdom. And we have no doubt that the strongest and most pervasive of these values is love. This chapter will explore why love is a fundamental principle for wise leaders, look at the relationship between love and caring, discuss leading from the heart, and see how a loving heart can light the way, energize our world, and express itself through compassion. From an infinite wellspring we will highlight the effects of love on ourselves, the people we lead, and our organizations.

Love Is a Fundamental Principle for Wise Leaders

Love is a fundamental principle for wise leaders because many of the archetypal principles we've identified have love as their foundation. The power of wise leadership is generated from love: love of doing good, love of doing the right thing, love of truth, love of justice, love of humankind, love of God, and so forth. God is love, the Bible tells us, but it is equally true that love is God. The energy of love and the energy of loving—in its purest form: unconditional, nonjudgmental, forgiving, and accepting—is a powerful force. From that perspective, love is the core principle from which flows everything that's good. A loving heart, an open heart, a heart that is generous and wants the best for the other person in all ways—all of these are fundamental to wise leadership. Wise leaders are incredibly empowering to their organizations.

You may be familiar with the song "Love Makes the World Go Round," from the 1961 musical *Carnival.* The song refers to the love between two people, but the same phrase serves as a metaphor for the divine energy that powers not only the trajectory of our world but also our hearts, both emotionally and spiritually. Once we experience the power of love and it becomes part of us, it's like lighting a wick on a candle. Each of us has a wick, and that wick is set aflame by a loving force. Then we have our own loving force. Once lit, it continues to burn brightly, and other people can be illuminated by our loving light. No matter how many times we use it, we still have a loving light that continues to ignite that wick in others. That's what wise leaders do.

Love Is the Highest Form of Caring

The leader of an organization, almost by definition, is intended to care about the organization and about the people in it. People in an organization want—*need*—a leader who has both a loving heart and a loving spirit. When you ask people about the kind of leader they would like to work for and work with, many wish for someone who has a loving heart, which is another way of saying "a caring person."

From our perspective, the source of that caring is love. That love may be conditional, or not as fully developed as it needs to be, or as powerful as it can be. But the source of a caring attitude toward others, and toward the organization, stems from that same flame of love we just described. Even though love is potentially inexhaustible, we must decide just how much of that loving energy we're willing to share and under what circumstances we're willing to share it. This is especially relevant in organizations that are responsible for the well-being of others, such as schools. Whenever Steve, as a superintendent of schools, met with prospective teachers he looked for a caring attitude about children. At a deeper level, he felt that if they displayed such a caring attitude, it came from the love within them. That was its source. It did not reside only in the mind, but in the heart. You can say, "I care about someone" from the vantage point of the mind, but when you care from the heart, that's when the source is love.

A Loving Heart Lights the Way

Certain people's hearts seem far bigger than normal. These folks—we've all come into contact with them at one time or another—are often described as having really big hearts, which is another way of saying that they have loving hearts. If you've noticed that about someone, other people have certainly noticed it too. It's not an attribute that can be kept secret somehow, or shown to some but not to others. It's just who they are.

Think for a moment about the way we react to a loving heart. We want to follow that loving heart. We want to be in the company of it, to bathe in its light and its energy. Love lights the way and provides an example to be followed. We've actually heard people say, "I'm not really sure that what is being proposed is a good idea, but if this person, our leader, is proposing it, I'm going to support it." This is one of the many ways in which leaders with loving hearts light the way for others.

Showing your love and light to people tells them the kind of person you are, but it also tells them about your connection to some higher power. People whose hearts are larger than their bodies are more in tune with the divine than others who may not be quite so capable of emanating that love. Such folks also have a kind of lightness to their being that makes them different from many of us. Everybody recognizes this energy when they come into contact with someone who manifests it. Such people change the vibration of everything around them. They are like a tuning fork for the rest of us; when they are present the energy shifts to a higher level. When you, as a leader, act as a tuning fork attuned to a higher power, you can shift the whole power of an organization, or a company, or a school system, or a country, or whatever you're leading.

Love Can Energize Our World

Love is a power that can energize us and the entire world. We see it as the highest form of energy, not in a physical sense but rather in a spiritual sense. Ultimately, love is the most powerful force there is.

Earlier we observed that the power of love is like kindling a flame that has the power to illuminate others. If each candle continues to light one other candle, within twenty iterations you will have more than a million lit candles. Continue, and the amount of energy and light becomes astronomical. This almost miraculous dynamic is not a zero-sum game. If I pass my light from my candle to yours, my candle still burns just as brightly as it did before I passed my light on to you; I have no less love than I had before. I didn't lose anything in the act of giving, the act of energizing.

Wise leaders are the ones who light the candle, create the fire. They are the source of love and loving energy in their organizations. The source of that light may be their own internal divine spark, or it may have been passed on to them by someone else, possibly a mentor or a parent.

Many of us have been fortunate enough to be mentored by other leaders. These people gave us their flame, passed their light on to us. Steve had two powerful mentors in his life; more than role models, they infused him with their love. When your candle is lit by someone who has a tremendous amount of love to give, that energy can sustain you for a lifetime. Wise leaders light the candles of countless others who, in turn, pass that light along during their lifetime. And the circle of light grows bigger and brighter as time goes on.

Leading from the Heart

The Myers-Briggs Personality Inventory (which was derived from the work of Carl Jung) makes it clear that in each person either the head or the heart dominates in decision making. In our experience leaders tend to be more head-centered than heart-centered. Wise leaders, however, need to be able to lead from both the heart and the head.

This is why it is appropriate at times for leaders to share experiences that convey and display their feelings to other people. People are more likely to trust someone who has had heartache, difficulties, and problems and who shares some of those experiences—a leader who can say, "I may be in a leadership position, but first and foremost, like you, I am a human being." People need to see in a leader someone who can share their pain and joy. They want to believe that their leaders have empathy, an understanding of what they're going through. How would you know such things about others if you have a heart of stone? People want to work for a leader who has a kind and loving heart.

Often, when people talk about a leader, they say that the person is "real." What does that mean? It signifies that they have made a connection with that person at a heart level. That person has revealed something personal in which others can see themselves. More commonly, CEOs and other people who run organizations have a tendency to put on their armor. They don their armor, helmets, and shields, and then they're all ready to face the world. But what does the world see? Someone encased in metal. And what is the world's first tendency? Let's see how thick that metal is! Let's see if we can poke a hole in it. Because all that's visible is a foreboding pseudoperson. You can't see the real face of the person under the hood or behind the mask. The wise leaders are the ones who take off the mask, take off the armor, expose themselves and their vulnerabilities, and say I *am* a person, I *am* a human, I *am* real. Cut me and I'll bleed just like you do. That kind of leadership has the power to forge a heart-level connection to people.

The More You Give Love, the More You Receive Love

If you don't believe that the more you give love the more you will receive it, then you see life as a zero-sum game. Your approach to life is going to be to husband your resources, hold back, use your love strategically, and apply it only when necessary. Operating in this manner amounts to shortchanging your organization. Though you have access to an infinite source of power, you are deciding to release only a little bit of your powerful potential at a time instead of turning on the juice all at once and lighting up the whole house. Wise leaders know that this source of energy is infinite and totally expansive. If you truly wish to light up an organization, turn on all on the power that's within you!

Here's another image: let's say that, as a leader, you generate love toward others in your organization in an open-hearted way. Over time your actions convey loving kindness both in the form of your practices and policies and in the way you interact with people, touching everyone in your organization in positive ways. When you kindle that sense of love in others, not only are they compelled to pass it along, but they're also naturally inclined to treat you in the same way. So you give out feelings of loving kindness in various forms, but that same loving kindness comes back amplified from all those with whom you interact. Even though our innate capacity to love is limitless, on a physical level we still need to be reenergized. The love that comes back energizes us not only physically but also spiritually. And ultimately our candle burns even brighter.

The opposite phenomenon is the Law of Expected Reciprocity and the Law of Unexpected Reciprocity. The Law of Expected Reciprocity says that the more you give out and expect back, the less you're going to get. The Law of Unexpected Reciprocity says that the more you give out and the less you expect back, the more you'll get back. It is in the giving and *not* expecting that you actually receive payback.

Why We Should Love Our Imperfect Selves

We need to love ourselves, not in a narcissistic way but in a way that truly values and appreciates our own uniqueness. Why is this important? Because you can't give what you don't have. You cannot love others unless you love yourself first, despite your shortcomings and imperfections. We are all imperfect. Wait to love yourself until you approach perfection and you're going to be waiting for a really long time. Truly loving ourselves, imperfect as we are, allows us to love others, imperfect as they are. If we hold ourselves to a standard close to perfection, then we are in danger of holding others to the same unreachable standard. From a leadership point of view, that's not a good thing.

We all make errors. Paul berates himself when he does something wrong. He does so to learn from his errors, not to punish himself. The internal dialogue goes something like this: "Well, you messed up, but you're not a perfect person. You're probably going to mess up again, but maybe you learned a lesson here." Paul does not dwell on his mistakes. He recognizes them, takes responsibility for them, and moves on. Steve's internal dialogue is a bit different: "Okay, I made an error, but I can still love myself. I'm a work in progress; God's not done with me yet." As leaders, we need to think of everyone in our organization as works in progress. God's not done with them either.

There's an interesting interplay here between expectation and forgiveness. At one level, leaders must hold very high expectations for those around them and communicate those expectations in a loving way, such as saying, "I really believe that you are capable of this high level of performance." At the same time, it's also necessary to be willing to forgive people if they fall short of meeting the standard. Sometimes people need another chance, or more time.

Someone once asked Steve, "How do you deal with failure?" Steve said, "I figure that I just need more time to get it right." Truly successful people understand that success and failure are so intertwined that it's almost meaningless to discuss them, because one often leads to the other. Turning failure into success has a lot to do with time, forgiveness, self-acceptance, and acceptance of the imperfection in each of us.

Why Acceptance Is an Important Element of the Serenity Prayer

Leaders are never satisfied with the status quo. They just naturally want to change things. They want to make things better. Sometimes the obstacles to be overcome seem insurmountable. Sometimes those obstacles truly *are* insurmountable, at least given current realities. Accepting that there are things we cannot change no matter how hard we try can be difficult for those of us who feel the need to find a way forward, no matter what. Like the cartoon character Pogo, we'd like to think that we are surrounded by insurmountable *opportunities* rather than insurmountable obstacles. Confronted with sorting out the difference, wise leaders sometimes reflect on the famous line from Reinhold Niebuhr's Serenity Prayer: "God grant me the serenity to accept the things I cannot change; courage to change the things I can; and wisdom to know the difference."

An aspect of the wisdom of wise leadership is not only knowing the right things to do, but also knowing what things you can affect and what things you probably cannot affect. Acceptance is an important ingredient, of course, but the wisdom to know when to accept circumstances and when to fight like hell is at the heart of the vantage point of a wise leader. From our perspective, even accepting that certain things cannot be changed doesn't mean you should not address them. Sometimes a leader makes a moral decision to fight for something even knowing that victory is not possible. Certain moral battles require a leader to take them on, even with the almost certain outcome of failure, just because it's the right thing to do. Even if the outcome is not what you had hoped for, your stance may still serve as a model for someone else, or contribute toward a much greater good because you took a moral stand.

How Leaders Can Let the Divine Light of Love Flow through Them

Paul and Steve believe in a higher power and believe that this higher power is the source and substance of the divine light of love. We also think it's important for leaders to acknowledge that the divine light of love exists. If you believe, as we do, that the divine light of love exists, then where is it? It's within us, in the form of pure potential. And if it is within us, then let it go—let it flow! Once you accept its potential for existing, you need the courage to let it out—by becoming a loving person, a loving leader. This decision takes faith because the act of becoming a loving person is in many ways an act of courage. You are stepping into the unknown because you have no idea what lies ahead or what the outcome will be.

As you practice being a loving person, a loving leader, the divine light of love within you grows stronger and stronger. And your desire to align yourself with that divine energy also grows stronger. One way of accelerating the process is to open yourself up to it. Think of yourself as a spigot or a pipe, and open yourself up so that divine love can flow through you. With your intention you can volunteer to be a conduit for sharing divine love.

We believe that human beings have free will. One exercise of that free will is the decision or choice that we make as to whether we wish to allow the divine light of love to flow through us. We have a choice about that. There are many approaches to opening ourselves up so that the divine light of love can flow through us and inform our decision making as leaders. You can use our metaphor of the spigot or pipe, prayer, visualization, chanting, dancing, or any method that works for you. One of the by-products of volunteering to be a channel for divine love is that as leaders our wisdom will surely grow, and we will get back what we give many times over.

To become The Wise Leaders:

- See love as a fundamental principle.
- See love as the highest form of caring.
- Know that a loving heart lights the way.
- Know that love can energize our world.
- Lead from the heart.
- Know that love creates compassion.
- Know that the wellspring of love is infinite.
- Know the more you give love the more you receive it.
- Know why we should love our imperfect selves.
- Know why acceptance is an important element of the Serenity Prayer.
- Let the divine light of love flow through you.

CHAPTER 18

The Wisdom of Forgiveness

Forgiveness? In a book on leadership? Surely forgiveness is a matter more fit for discussion in the church or temple. Leadership is a dance between the leader and the led, however, and if the music is off, the dance falters. And forgiveness is at the heart of that dance. Thus it is a core principle for leaders.

Forgiveness clears the deck; it cuts away the underbrush that blocks forward progress. Failing to forgive means that you're holding on to the past and remaining stuck with what has happened in the past, which blocks you from seeing what is possible ahead of you. Failing to forgive is like dumping the contents of your garbage can in the middle of the living room. You're cluttering and stinking up your life. You cannot establish any sort of new relationship with the person you are refusing to forgive; you're left, instead, with a big backpack of stones you carry with you constantly. Think of it—it's hard to walk, and certainly impossible to run, when you're carrying such a heavy load, just as it's hard to enjoy life with a pile of garbage sitting in the middle of your living space. And it is impossible for an organization to flourish if it's burdened with a multitude of unresolved issues from the past.

The great irony of forgiveness, whether personal or organizational, is that it's not about the party who has offended or hurt you—it's about *you*. The act of forgiveness lightens the burden of the forgiver. Often it may have no impact whatsoever on the one who is being forgiven. In fact, the person who has been forgiven rarely knows that it happened. They may not even know they did something that needed forgiving! *We are the ones who create the hurt we feel.* They will live their life just as they did before forgiveness was offered or withheld. But the quality of the life of the one who forgives is markedly improved because the forgiver no longer has that burden to carry.

So many people believe that by forgiving they are letting the other person off the hook somehow. Actually, the other person was never *on* the hook. He was either unaware of what he did or simply didn't care that he might have hurt you. Will not forgiving him change his behavior? Probably not. Our main reason for not forgiving others is our own need to be right or to see ourselves as right. Understand that the act of forgiving does not make you wrong. It just allows the other person to have been wrong. Not forgiving others changes *our* behavior; it makes us bitter and angry.

Moreover, holding on to anger and hurt is corrosive and toxic; it debilitates the person holding on to the anger. The irony here is that all that is required to forgive is to say, or even think, words of forgiveness. Forgiveness doesn't cost money or reputation or take anything away from the one doing the forgiving. It's simply a matter of you releasing your feelings. Doesn't seem as if it should be that hard—but for many of us it can sometimes seem impossible.

Paul was brought up by a person who found it very hard to forgive. She held on to every slight and hurt; her holding on to hurts made her bitter, caused her to dwell on the past, and blocked her happiness because the hurts were always lurking just below the surface. The quality of her life suffered because she was deeply invested in being right and seeing those who had hurt her as wrong. Sadly, she never understood that she could be right and still forgive the other person. Forgiveness isn't about surrendering to the other person—it's about surrendering your ego and your need to feel righteous and allowing yourself to move on. The interesting thing is that she was a very religious person and taught Paul about forgiveness. She understood the *theory* of forgiveness; she just couldn't get to the core of it. She would sometimes ask Paul how he could be so forgiving toward someone who had hurt him. He would laugh and say, "Because that's what you taught me!" But while she understood the concept of forgiveness from her time in church, she didn't comprehend its essence.

The same is true for an organization. If the leader fails to forgive, and does not promote forgiveness, then those in the organization are likely to replay what has happened (and can no longer be changed) rather than to seek new solutions. Likewise, an organization can be poisoned by an inability to move ahead from past issues. This kind of toxic environment can cripple and even kill an organization. It blocks people from working together, it blocks communication, and it stifles creative problem solving.

Organizations must move forward; to do so they must sometimes wipe the slate clean and start anew without having to settle who was right or wrong. Paul was in England a few years ago when the British soccer team lost in the World Cup competition. The Brits had been expected to win. Within moments of the end of the game, the media started a barrage of "Who's to blame?" stories. The stories arose from a deep need to pin responsibility for the failure on *someone*. The loss consumed the country for days. But did all that recrimination help the British win the next World Cup? Of course not. It didn't even make them feel better! Sometimes it's necessary to let things go so you can move forward.

One staff member in Paul's organization was so upset with another that she couldn't get any work done. In his mediation of the conflict Paul saw that trying to untangle who was right and who was wrong would be impossible, so he simply suggested that the two of them forgive each other. After a moment of stunned silence one of them said, "Well, we might as well—we don't know what else to do." Forgiveness was the last resort. A lot of time and energy would have been saved if it had been the first response.

It all comes down to the right to choose. All of us have the right to choose forgiveness. Forgiveness is not a magical formula. It's a practical response to a lot of psychic trouble. You just decide to do it, and in that moment of decision, it is done.

Compassionate Leadership and Forgiveness

It's good to remember that every organization is made up of human beings. And human beings are subject to failure. Everyone in any organization will do things at some point that others will find offensive or hurtful or lacking. When you get to the core of things, organizations are really just a collection of interpersonal relationships. Therefore, the need for forgiveness always exists. If the leader is unforgiving and uncompassionate, the result is weak leadership and a poor organization. One of any leader's core roles is (or should be) delegation. If you cannot forgive someone for not doing something exactly the way that you would, however, you can never delegate effectively.

Today's organizations rise and fall on their ability to be creative. And organizations need people who are able to think outside the box and find new ways of doing things. But if you desire an entrepreneurial atmosphere you must create a *forgiving* atmosphere. The only way people can create is by trying and failing. If you frown on failure, then clearly you don't want people to try. The fastest way to stop striving within an organization is to punish failure. If we punish failure the lesson learned is not to try. Whether it be in a classroom or a company, you want people to take risks, to stretch themselves, to push beyond their boundaries, to go where they haven't gone before. The only way to make this happen in an organization is to create an atmosphere in which taking a risk is safe, even if you don't succeed.

Understand, though, that responsibility and accountability are also necessary. The secret of real accountability is that it creates a base for forward progress. If there is too much punishment, there is no reason to try. We acknowledge the error or failure, focus on what can be learned from it, and move forward.

Leaders Must Learn to Forgive Themselves

It is impossible to forgive someone else unless you can forgive yourself. You cannot be compassionate to others if you are not compassionate to yourself. Let us stipulate right now that each of us is a defective, damaged, wayward person—a human, in other words. Given that reality, we must start from a willingness to forgive ourselves for being imperfect.

Leaders, by definition, are achievers. We got to be leaders by being successful. But we need to remember that we didn't get to success by being successful *all* the time. We got there by learning from our mistakes. In essence, making mistakes was one of the most important things we did to nurture our success. So it shouldn't be that hard to say to ourselves, "You know, it's okay. I forgive you for being less than perfect."

If you are a perfectionist it can be very hard to forgive imperfection—particularly in yourself. If you allow yourself to get hung up on your own failures, however, you'll never be able to move forward. Wise leaders understand that the pursuit of perfection leads to greatness. But they also understand that perfection is impossible to achieve, so they accept that trying to achieve it and falling short is okay. Think of it as the Scarlett O'Hara model of leadership: "Tomorrow is another day." All of us are constantly being presented with opportunities to turn things around and do better. Wise leaders understand the complex interplay between perfectionism and forgiveness.

Wise leaders also understand that we humans are all works in progress. God isn't through with us yet. It can be hard to accept that not only do we make great mistakes while striving for greatness but we also sometimes make dumb or silly mistakes doing the mundane! Again and again, it seems, we take a wrong road, or make a wrong call, or do something that in hindsight looks downright stupid. We have come to regard these foul-ups as part of our training in staying humble, for—regardless of our training, education, and experience— invariably we are going to make mistakes. Sometimes we are the only ones who know what we have done. Other times, unfortunately, our errors are spectacularly public ones. The more public the mistake, the more public its acknowledgment must be. A tip: it helps to focus on the word "error" rather than on the notion of "right" or "wrong." Most commonly, errors have nothing to do with the realm of moral judgment. But bringing the notion of right or wrong into play implies judgment. We all make errors and we understand that errors call for correction—they do not call for condemnation.

Once the members of Steve's leadership staff were complaining about people coming to work late. They instituted a system in which the sign-in sheet was changed at 8:02 on the dot so that they could tell exactly who was on time and who was late. They quickly realized, however, that the new system was certainly catching employees who were "guilty" of arriving at work a minute or three late, but many of those same culprits had worked late (and sometimes *very* late) the previous day. In other words, the new system was punishing the wrong people for the errors of a few. Steve rescinded the policy he had recently approved, acknowledged the mistake publicly, and spoke of the importance of trusting the staff to do what was right. If a few people could not do the right thing, he added, they would be dealt with separately. All he had really done was to admit an error publicly, but employees at every level were so impressed by his public gesture that enormous good will resulted.

One time Paul took over the leadership of a very large urban school system that had been fraught with racial tension. His hiring, as a Caucasian, had only fueled the tension. Many in the community were just waiting for his first mistake. He obliged them by making a joke that, in reality, was quite benign but provided sufficient ammunition to those who were out to get him. They wrote Paul a letter excoriating him for his mistake, and it was leaked to the newspaper before he even received it. In some ways he had simply walked into the trap that had been set for him. If his lame attempt at humor had not triggered the public outburst, something else surely would have. As Paul was licking his wounds, one of his staff members gave him some sound advice. The staff member suggested that, instead of focusing on the unfairness of the incident, Paul make a public apology.

Paul's response was typical Paul: "What do you mean 'apologize'? I'm not the one who's wrong here!"

Another staff member replied, "Yep, you're right. Now go out and apologize."

Paul realized that his staff was right. The reaction to Paul's public apology was dramatic. People in the community were shocked. They had become so accustomed to back-and-forth fighting in the district that when Paul simply took responsibility for the issue, the matter was ended. All the negative energy evaporated. It is perhaps a sad commentary that when a leader apologizes for a mistake—as both Steve and Paul did—his simple but powerful act elicits such a dramatic response. That suggests that it happens too rarely.

Admitting an error and apologizing is a terrific way of defusing issues and putting them behind you. Mistakes made and not acknowledged simmer and eventually boil over. Negative energy only becomes greater. Any apology must be authentic, of course. People know insincerity when they see it.

Have you noticed how many apologies lately have taken this form: "I apologize if you were offended." That wording actually places the blame on those to whom you're apologizing! What it really says is, "Sorry you were so dumb as to be offended by my perfectly innocent remark." How about just saying that you're sorry (if you truly are) and moving on. That has the ring of authenticity. Most times, when you take responsibility for a mistake and ask for forgiveness, the offended or affected party will accept your apology, creating a sense of closure. But if they do not accept your apology, remember that it wasn't for them anyway—it was for you.

It's useful to think of forgiveness as a gift. You can't force someone to give you the gift of forgiveness, and they can't force you to offer it to them. Forgiveness is a gift that must be freely given and freely accepted. If your request for forgiveness is refused, the breach has not been closed, but you have lightened the burden on yourself and offered to lighten it for the other person.

We've all heard people say, "I can forgive, but I will never forget." Let's face it: what that *really* means is "I say I forgive you, but I'm going to hold on to my feelings anyway." You cannot forgive halfway. Either you forgive or you do not forgive. Obviously you cannot erase whatever happened from your memory, but the way you feel about it and respond emotionally will tell you whether you have really forgiven.

It's helpful to think of forgiveness as a way of getting to the heart of things. Forgiveness is not a puzzle that the brain can solve; it must come from the heart. You can talk yourself into thinking you have forgiven someone, but if you haven't let the matter go in your heart, then forgiveness has not happened. And you don't want to risk damaging your heart by allowing it to remain full of anger and recrimination.

Forgiveness Releases the Bonds of Negative Energy

The absence of forgiveness creates a downward spiral that leads from one negative point to another until ultimately a point of no return is reached. When you fail to forgive, the negative energy that you hold and express is received, magnified, and returned to you. The only way to break this cycle and reverse the flow of negative energy is to forgive. Forgiveness becomes the difference between creativity and growth or a potentially dangerous escalation of negativity.

A lack of forgiveness creates a bond of negative energy. But why would you wish to hold on to negative energy and feed it?

Such energy, since it touches both the sender and the receiver, can be toxic both for the one needing to forgive and the one being forgiven. When you allow negative energy to be a part of you, you sacrifice much of your ability to create positive energy. Moreover, the negative effects can spill over into other parts of your life. In fact, the downward spiral of negative energy caused by holding on to anger and hurt can be much more harmful than the original negative act that caused the hurt. Molehills really do become mountains! A small act of hurtfulness can spiral and grow into something ugly and pernicious. The notorious feud between the Hatfields and the McCoys began with the killing of a pig and ended up ravaging two extended families.

Paul visualizes the failure to forgive, and the act of holding on to the hurt and anger we feel, as a heavy stone we pick up. We can then choose to carry that stone with us always, or to put it down. The longer we hold on to the stone, the heavier it becomes. At first, when something bad happens to you or someone hurts you, it's easy to remember and resent the incident. The longer you carry those feelings around with you, however, the bigger and heavier they become; it takes more and more energy to hold on to them. Far better to say, "Stone, I will not carry you," and drop your burden.

Forgiveness Allows Us to Begin Anew

Forgiveness is the only way to sever the cords that can bind us to the past. Sometimes we can become so engrossed in things that people did to us directly, or even indirectly, that we forget that the issue took place in the past and cannot be changed. Why allow something you can't change to dictate your happiness in the present? Part of forgiveness is forgiving the past and letting it go.

Educators (and both Steve and Paul are career educators) are very fortunate because each school year is a clean slate. Teachers have the opportunity to start over with a new group of children each year; they can improve upon what they did the previous year.

And just as schools have rituals that involve new beginnings, some religions have different rituals and traditions that allow people to atone for the past and move forward. The Jewish faith has Yom Kippur, which allows adherents to forgive themselves and others for anything that happened during the previous year. Catholics have the tradition of confession that allows them to confess their shortcomings and be absolved of them. Ramadan serves a similar purpose for Muslims. Christians believe that Christ died for their sins and that, through God's grace, they are forgiven for their trespasses.

On the secular side, we celebrate the New Year and its tradition of resolutions to allow a new beginning. (Of course, the tradition of getting drunk and acting foolish on New Year's Eve isn't the best way to start!) But it's not necessary to subscribe to a specific faith to begin anew. You just have to forgive, both yourself and others, for what has happened in the past.

Forgiveness Is Liberating

The act of forgiveness relieves you of a great weight, creating a sense of lightness and possibility. Anger, on the other hand—whether you're facing the anger of others or expressing it yourself—rarely seems to clear things up. Instead, anger seems only to add to the difficulty of whatever situation you were facing in the first place.

Once Paul found himself in a situation in which a person was out to get him. The constant barrage of accusations and criticism he faced created a feeling of heaviness. He even found himself walking more slowly, as if he carried a great load on his shoulders (which of course he did). He could see no solution, no way out. So Paul did what he always tries to do: he released the matter, letting go of his feelings toward the other person and the entire situation. In the Christian tradition, this act is known as "surrender," but not surrender in the sense of giving up. Rather, you give over. You surrender to the situation and its possibilities. When Paul surrendered he could feel himself changed. He no longer felt weighed down; he felt free—and he *was* free. The entire situation lightened right away. Ironically, the person who had been causing him trouble got in trouble himself, and life moved forward.

Knowing that forgiveness is liberating, leaders always have the choice to create a sense of liberation for themselves and others. You can be the injured party or you can be the injuring party. You can be the nail or the hammer. Or you can choose to be the welder who binds the pieces together. Whatever the situation, the leader has the power to initiate the solution. You do that by forgiving yourself, forgiving others, and letting go of the past.

Obviously, leadership is a tough job; it comes with heavy responsibilities. Leaders need to model high standards and expectations. We set the tone and through our example give permission for others to behave in the same way we do. Leaders are accountable for the success of their organization; they have to hold others accountable. Ideally, the system of accountability is fair and understood by all. Forgiveness is not a pardon or absolution, however. There can still be consequences for an error. What really matters, though, is how the leader and the one being led feel about the interaction. After all,

245

there will be other days with other expectations, and the way in which the relationship between the parties is handled is what matters in the long run.

Love Is the Foundation for Forgiveness

Just as love is the foundation for forgiveness, forgiveness is the foundation for love. Forgiveness is the act of a loving heart.

Consider this challenging example: during one of Paul's superintendencies, he faced the problem of a department head that was guilty of making major errors that had the potential to jeopardize the entire organization. After giving the department head several chances to correct the situation, with no results, Paul felt he had to dismiss the person. He tried his best to let the person know that while her work did not meet expectations, Paul still considered her a worthy person. Paul tried to speak straight from his heart and with a sense of dedication to the person's soul. At the end of the conversation the person being dismissed thanked Paul and hugged him.

Paul had managed to convey that he was acting not only in the best interest of the organization but also in the best interest of the employee. In so doing, Paul had expressed heart leadership. He had shown that he forgave the employee for the shortcomings of her department and that he cared about her as a person. That type of action should be the goal for anyone who has the responsibility for any organization and for the people in it. To the degree that you can operate with a loving heart, you shortcut the need for forgiveness within the organization. It is when we drift from that place of love that things begin to go bad. It is important to try to separate the act from the person. Yes, her department had failed, but that did not make her a failure or mean that she could not be successful next time. She was still a valued and valuable person.

The bottom line is that forgiveness is a powerful force, as is the love that undergirds it. The two forces, acting together, have the power to transform the lives of those we lead. Paul, as a Christian, has always scoffed at the image some hold of Christ as a weak, unrealistic soul who walked the earth dispensing the idea of love and was crucified for his efforts. Instead, from all accounts, Jesus was so strong that he was able to forgive those who crucified him as it was happening. Most of us will never meet that standard. But we can work toward creating a greater sense of forgiveness in the workplace we lead and in our life and the lives of those with whom we interact each day. The force of love and heart is so much more powerful than the force of head and hate. Real leadership starts with the heart and moves outward and upward from there.

To become The Wise Leader:

- **Know that forgiveness is central to what you do.**
- **Know that compassionate leadership requires forgiveness.**
- **Know that you must forgive yourself first.**
- **Know that it is important to admit error and to apologize.**
- **Know that forgiveness releases the bonds of negative energy.**
- **Know that forgiveness allows us to begin anew.**
- **Know that forgiveness is liberating.**
- **Know that love is the foundation of forgiveness.**

Conclusion

We hope you found *The Wise Leader* enlightening, empowering, and imbued with wisdom. The following principles and values we illuminated are seeds of wisdom:

- Our unique life lessons
- Revering all living beings
- Focusing on the positive
- Trust
- Walking the talk
- Fighting for what's right
- Understanding that light attracts the dark
- Balance
- Empowering and uplifting others
- Synergy
- Attention
- Having an attitude of gratitude
- Focusing on the now
- Serving others
- Operating from a base of compassion
- Hope over fear
- Love
- Forgiveness

You might find it useful to sort this list into three groups, focusing on one group at a time during each of the next three years. If you focus on each principle within the group for a two-month period, you could incorporate all of them into your style of leadership over a three-year timeframe. Every two months reread the chapter you're focusing on, including the "To become The Wise Leader" section at the end of the chapter. Commit to putting the principle into action, formulate and carry through on a plan to do so, and watch what happens.

As you nurture these seeds of wisdom you will make wiser choices and you'll increasingly become The Wise Leader—a leader who does the right things for the right reasons.

We have formed a center that serves as an information network, a support network, and a forum for collaboration and training for people who are striving to become wise leaders.

Share your experiences with us at www.cfel.org. Sign up for our triannual e-newsletter/journal *The Lens*. If you would like us to conduct seminars or training for you or your staff in the practice of these principles, you can reach us at the e-mail addresses below. Wise leadership is the path to a better and brighter future for us all.

Sincerely,
Stephen L. Sokolow (SLsokolow@aol.com)
Paul D. Houston (phouston@eddsnet.com)

About the Authors

Dr. Paul D. Houston
phouston@eddsnet.com

Dr. Paul D. Houston, former executive director of the American Association of School Administrators, has established himself as one of the leading spokespersons for American education through his extensive speaking engagements, published articles, and his regular appearances on national radio and television. He is currently coauthoring a series of books on wise leadership and is president and a founding partner of the Center for Empowered Leadership.

Dr. Houston served schools in North Carolina, New Jersey, and Alabama prior to serving as superintendent of schools in Princeton, New Jersey; Tucson, Arizona; and Riverside, California.

Dr. Houston has also served in an adjunct capacity for the University of North Carolina, Harvard University, Brigham Young University, and Princeton University. He has served as a consultant and speaker throughout the United States and internationally, and he has published more than 150 articles in professional journals.

Dr. Houston completed his undergraduate degree at The Ohio State University, received his master's degree at the University of North Carolina, and earned a Doctorate of Education from Harvard University.

In 1991, Dr. Houston was honored for his leadership in urban education when he received the Richard R. Green Leadership Award from the Council of the Great City Schools. In 1997, he was awarded an honorary Doctorate of Education from Duquesne University. The Hope Foundation honored Dr. Houston with the Courageous Leadership Award of 2000. The Horace Mann League presented Dr. Houston with the league's 2001 Outstanding Educator Award, citing him as an articulate spokesperson for strong and effective public education. Dr. Houston coauthored the book *Exploding the Myths*, published in 1993, and in 1997 published *Articles of Faith & Hope for Public Education*. In 2004, he published *Perspectives on American Education*. Dr. Houston coauthored *The Spiritual Dimension of Leadership* in 2006. And in 2010 he authored *Giving Wings to Children's Dreams*.

Dr. Houston is committed to advocacy for public education and the children it serves.

Dr. Stephen L. Sokolow
SLsokolow@aol.com

Dr. Stephen L. Sokolow, a former superintendent of schools, is currently coauthoring a series of books on wise leadership. He is also a founding partner and executive director of the Center for Empowered Leadership.

Dr. Sokolow served schools in Pennsylvania and Delaware prior to serving as superintendent of schools in the Upper Freehold Regional School District in Monmouth County, New Jersey, and the Bridgewater-Raritan Regional School District in Somerset County, New Jersey.

Dr. Sokolow completed his undergraduate degree and master's degree at Temple University, where he also earned a doctorate of education. He was awarded several fellowships and later served in Temple's Department of Educational Leadership as an adjunct professor. He is a past president of the Temple University Educational Administration Doctoral Alumni Association.

He is past president of the Superintendents' Roundtable in Monmouth County, New Jersey. From 1986 through 2001, he participated in the Harvard University summer invitational seminar for superintendents. Dr. Sokolow represented the superintendents of Somerset County, New Jersey, as a member of the New Jersey Association of School Administrators Executive Committee and served as a member of the New Jersey Governor's Task Force on Education.

In 1986, Dr. Sokolow was selected by *Executive Educator*, a publication of the National School Boards Association, as one of the top one hundred small-district school executives in North America. He was honored for his leadership as a superintendent by the New Jersey Legislature in 1987 and was profiled by *The School Administrator*, a national publication of the American Association of School Administrators, for his "outside--the-box thinking" in January 1999.

His feature article on "Enlightened Leadership" was published in September 2002 in *The School Administrator*, as was his November 2005 article on "Nourishing Our Spirit as Leaders." Dr. Sokolow coauthored *The Spiritual Dimension of Leadership* in 2006. In 2008, he was a contributor to *Spirituality in Educational Leadership* as part of the Soul of Educational Leadership series.

Dr. Sokolow is a child-centered educator committed to empowering wise leadership in both the public and private sectors, but especially in the field of education.

Selected Bibliography

Albom, Mitch. *Tuesdays with Morrie.* New York: Doubleday, 1997.

Bolman, Lee G., and Terrence E. Deal, *Leading with Soul.* San Francisco: Jossey-Bass, 1995.

Bronowski, Jacob. *The Ascent of Man.* Boston: Little, Brown, 1973.

Bruyere, Rosalyn L. *Wheels of Light.* New York: Fireside, 1989.

Campbell, Joseph. *The Power of Myth.* New York: Doubleday, 1988.

Chambers, Shirley. *Kabalistic Healing.* Los Angeles: Keats, 2000.

Chopra, Deepak. *Ageless Body, Timeless Mind.* New York: Crown, 1994.

Chopra, Deepak. *The Seven Spiritual Laws of Success.* San Rafael, CA: Amber-Allen, 1994.

Collins, Jim. *Good to Great.* New York: HarperCollins, 2001.

Covey, Stephen R. *Principle-Centered Leadership.* New York: Summit Books, 1990.

Crichton, Michael. *Travels.* New York: Ballantine, 1988.

Crum, Thomas F. *The Magic of Conflict.* New York: Simon & Schuster, 1987.

Dyer, Wayne W. *Real Magic.* New York: Harper, 1992.

Dyer, Wayne W. *Wisdom of the Ages.* New York: Avon Books, 1998.

Dyer, Wayne W. *There's a Spiritual Solution to Every Problem.* New York: HarperCollins, 2001.

Dyer, Wayne W. *The Power of Intention.* Carlsbad, CA: Hay House, 2004.

Farson, Richard. *Management of the Absurd.* New York: Simon & Schuster, 1996.

Ferguson, Marilyn. *The Aquarian Conspiracy.* Boston: Houghton Mifflin, 1980.

Fullan, Michael. *Leading in a Culture of Change.* San Francisco: Jossey-Bass, 2001.

Gawain, Shakti. *Creative Visualization.* New York: MJF Books, 1978.

Gladwell, Malcolm. *Blink.* New York: Little, Brown, 2005.

Gleick, James. *Chaos.* New York: Penguin, 1987.

Greene, Brian. *The Elegant Universe.* New York: W. W. Norton, 1999.

Hawking, Stephen. *The Universe in a Nutshell.* New York: Bantam Books, 2001.

Hawkins, David R. *Power vs. Force.* Carlsbad, CA: Hay House, 2002.

Heider, John. *The Tao of Leadership.* New York: Bantam Books, 1986.

Hoyle, John R. *Leadership and the Force of Love.* Thousand Oaks, CA: Sage, 2001.

Jackson, Phil. *Sacred Hoops.* New York: Hyperion, 1995.

Jaworski, Joseph. *Synchronicity: The Inner Path of Leadership.* San Francisco: Berrett-Koehler, 1996.

Kessler, Rachael. *The Soul of Education.* Alexandria, VA: Association for Supervision and Curriculum Development, 2000.

Lenz, Frederick. *Surfing the Himalayas.* New York: St. Martin's, 1995.

Markova, Dawna. *The Smart Parenting Revolution.* New York: Random House, 2005.

Millman, Dan. *Way of the Peaceful Warrior.* Tiburon, CA: H. J. Kramer, 1980.

Millman, Dan. *The Life You Were Born to Live.* Tiburon, CA: H. J. Kramer, 1993.

Myss, Caroline. *Anatomy of the Spirit.* New York: Harmony, 1996.

Myss, Caroline. *Sacred Contracts.* New York: Random House, 2003.

Nouwen, Henri J. M. *The Return of the Prodigal Son.* New York: Doubleday, 1992.

Peck, M. Scott. *The Road Less Traveled.* New York: Simon & Schuster, 1978.

Peters, Thomas J., and Robert H. Waterman. *In Search of Excellence.* New York: Harper & Row, 1982.

Ponce, Charles. *Kabbalah.* Adyar, Chennai, India: Theosophical Publishing House, 1991.

Quinn, Daniel. *Ishmael.* New York: Bantam, 1995.

Redfield, James. *The Celestine Prophecy.* New York: Warner, 1993.

Redfield, James. *The Tenth Insight.* New York: Warner, 1996.

Redfield, James. *The Secret of Shambhala.* New York: Warner, 1999.

Remen, Rachel Naomi. *My Grandfather's Blessings.* New York: Riverhead Books, 2000.

Ruiz, Don Miguel. *The Four Agreements.* San Rafael, CA: Amber-Allen, 1997.

Schiller, Marjorie, Bea Mah Holland, and Deanna Riley, eds. *Appreciative Leaders: In the Eye of the Beholder.* Chagrin Falls, OH: Taos Institute, 2001.

Senge, Peter, et al. *Presence.* Cambridge, MA: Society for Organizational Learning, 2004.

Sharamon, Shalila, and Bodo Baginski. *The Chakra Handbook.* Wilmot, WI: Lotus Light, 1991.

Simpson, Liz. *The Book of Chakra Healing.* New York: Sterling, 1999.

Thompson, Scott. *Leading from the Eye of the Storm.* Lanham, MD: Rowman & Littlefield Education, 2005.

Waitley, Denis. *Seeds of Greatness.* New York: Simon & Schuster, 1983.

Wheatley, Margaret J. *Leadership and the New Science.* San Francisco: Berrett-Koehler, 1992.

Wilkinson, Bruce. *The Prayer of Jabez*. Sisters, OR: Multnomah, 2000.

Zukav, Gary. *The Seat of the Soul*. New York: Fireside, 1989.

Zukav, Gary. *Soul Stories*. New York: Simon & Schuster, 2000.